Testimonials from Dreams Interpreted Using the Dreamtime Method

"Your dream interpretation was exact. One would think that you have been residing in my head hearing my private dialogue with myself. I just wanted to say how right on you were. I will try to follow my 'best friend's' advice. Thank you again." —*Yolanda L.*

"May I truly say that I was totally amazed at the interpretation. I had no idea that the symbols in my dream were anything other than what I consciously knew them to be. In other words, I thought I was having some kind of sexual fantasy. Your interpretation was not only refreshing and peaked my interest further, but it was right on the money. I'm still a little in shock over what you said, but this is a good thing. I really want to know more because I feel as though I am just seeing the tip of the iceberg with so much more to reveal! I cannot thank you enough for your insight. Now I want to go to bed to dream and then find out how to interpret my dreams for myself. The secrets in my mind are what I am dying to find out." —*Todd D.*

"I found your interpretation not only uncanny in its accuracy, but fascinating in terms of method. It truly was pertinent to the biggest issue in my life right now, how to make a commitment to my poetry writing. Is there some way that I might learn your method? I have browsed through various kinds of books ranging from ridiculous 'dream symbol dictionaries' to more intuitive, intelligent approaches. Your particular approach seems to lend credibility to the process! I was amazed that you could tap into my reality through this sketchy, barely remembered dream that I sent to you as an impulsive whim! Thanks for your great response and I look forward to talking to you again!" —*Aviva K.*

"Well, thank you very much. The dream was extremely insightful. In fact, much of what you said related to decisions that I am dealing with in my life in terms of direction. I was surprised that you returned the dream message so soon! Thank you, you were a big help and made me realize where my focus needs to be." —*Caramel M.*

"I want to thank you for your wonderfully insightful dream interpretation readings you have done for me. I have been on a path to creating a project on a global scale and the dreams I have been having, as you have shown me, were all about the process. Your interpretation and methods were perfect and in alignment with my own projections and goals. You were able to supply a piece to the puzzle that has kept me moving in the right direction and navigating around obstacles I would have never seen. Thank you so much." —*Nancy C.*

Dreamtime
Dream Interpretation

Opening to Your Spiritual Sight Within

Terri Ullstrup

Dreamtime Publishing
Westminster, Colorado

Dreamtime Dream Interpretation
Opening to Your Spiritual Sight Within
by Terri Ullstrup

Published by:
Dreamtime Publishing
Westminster, CO 80021 USA
www.dreaminterpretation.com

ISBN 978-0-9672716-1-3

Publisher's Cataloging-in-Publication Data
Ullstrup, Terri.
Dreamtime dream interpretation : opening to your
spiritual sight within / Terri Ullstrup.
p. cm.
Includes index.
LCCN 2009909204
ISBN-13: 9780967271613
ISBN-10: 0967271614

1. Dream interpretation.   I. Title.

BF1091.U45 2009   154.6'3
QBI09-600237

This book was manufactured in the United States of America.

I dedicate this book to my husband Dave . . . who I love to "pieces."

To my beloved animal companions and guides: Auggie, Sundance, Saydrah and Cody.

I also dedicate this work to Mother Earth, Father Sun and Mother Sky.
And to all energy of this Universe and beyond and beyond . . .

We are here.
We are whole.
We are one.
We are healed, complete . . . and free.

And to Knowing Dreamers All.

Acknowledgments

I want to thank my family, my sisters, brothers and my Mom for all of their love, support and encouragement to write this book.

I want to thank Robert Aulicino, who helped me create the beautiful cover of this book and was very patient with me in all ways of putting this book together. I want to thank Robin Quinn, my Editor, who really helped me focus on what it is I wanted to communicate and was so encouraging. I especially want to thank Jeff Copp, a gifted friend, who always was there when I needed him to assist with the production of this book.

*"Humanity must never cease to dream.
Dreams are stronger than the sword."*
Robert Muller

Terri's Dream

In my dream, standing in front of me, was a very tall, thin and hard-looking man. He was staring at me deeply with his severe eyes. I felt as though he was some sort of regal, authority figure, as he was dressed in robes that were of a yellow color. The feeling I got from him as he stared at me was that I had better not get out of line or the punishment would be severe. He was an ugly man who made me feel absolute fear.

I then felt a presence behind me. I did not turn around as I didn't know if I should. The presence wrapped its arms or wings around my whole body from behind, and the wings or arms totally enveloped me. I then felt the deepest, most ecstatic feeling of love that I have ever experienced. I remember that feeling to this day, as I have never felt it again. It was like some sort of unbelievable, beautiful feeling of being protected with a love of pure bliss!

This loving presence then communicated to me:

Take your love and light to Earth with you now . . .

and then bring it back home again.

Reader: I dreamed this dream many years ago, at the beginning of my exploration of dream interpretation. I never felt before nor have felt since such deep totally encompassing love. But I remember it so well and the message the presence gave to me. Finally, now with this book, I have the opportunity to share my love and light with you through the Dreamtime Method. Thank you!

Dream Interpretation leads you to Enlightenment as it shows you how . . .

You are the Creator that is creating your life.

How to Use This Book

Your *Dreamtime Dream Interpretation* book first introduces you to your own DreamSelf, the multi-dimensional part of you that creates your dreams for you. This book then goes on to easily teach you how to *think multi-dimensionally* as your DreamSelf Within (the Dreamtime Method) to accurately interpret your dreams.

Chapter One: The Magician, Your DreamSelf Within

★ Chapter One introduces you to your DreamSelf Within, the magical, multi-dimensional part of yourself within that creates your dreams for you. You meet this exciting part of yourself within and begin to understand how extraordinary and multi-dimensional you (and your dreams) are!

Chapter Two: The Foundation of Interpreting Your Dreams Accurately—Understanding Yourself as a Multi-Dimensional Energy Being

★ In Chapter Two, you learn to understand yourself as a Multi-dimensional Energy Being. You are given an overview of how to think multi-dimensionally with easy graphics to visualize the process. You learn how your multi-dimensional dream energy as *living energy* creates your three-dimensional Self and life. You learn the origins of your extraordinary DreamSelf Within.

Chapters Three through Seven of *Dreamtime Dream Interpretation* explain my easy to learn and use step-by-step method of how to interpret your dreams multi-dimensionally and accurately (the Dreamtime Method).

Chapter Three: Learning the Dreamtime Method and Tapping into Your Dreamtime Consciousness Within

★ In Chapter Three, you learn your DreamSelf's thinking and consciousness which is your Spiritual Sight Within. In this chapter, you will be introduced to the specifics of the Dreamtime Method (multi-dimensional thinking). You learn to interpret each of your dream symbols using the Dreamtime Method and are given an easy to use Dreamtime Method Dream Symbol Template Form. Many dream symbols examples with graphics are given in this chapter to familiarize and teach you how to easily use the Dreamtime Method to interpret your individual dream symbols from your dream. You will also learn to create your own Dreamtime Dictionary of dream symbols.

Chapter Four: Interpreting Your Written Dream Using the Dreamtime Method

★ Chapter Four teaches you how to keep a Dream Journal. In this chapter, you will also learn to use the Dreamtime Method to interpret each of your dream symbols and then how to add them together to get the complete thoughts of your DreamSelf from your whole written down dream.

Chapter Five: Interpreting Common Dream Themes Using the Dreamtime Method

★ In Chapter Five, I interpret common dreams themes using the Dreamtime Method with an understanding of why these dream themes so commonly occur in your dreams. This chapter allows you to review how to use the Dreamtime Method to interpret your own dreams. Dream themes included are: recurring-repeat dreams, nightmare dreams, chase dreams, death dreams, other people you know dreams, sex dreams, cleansing dreams and animal-insect dreams.

Chapter Six: Dreamtime Extras! Interpreting Numbers & Alphabet Letters, Techniques for Remembering & Programming Your Dreams, and How to Use the Dreamtime Dreamwheel

★ In Chapter Six, you will learn to use the Dreamtime Method to interpret numbers and alphabet letters that we all see in our dreams as dreams symbols. You will learn techniques for remembering and programming your dreams that work! You will then learn how to use your Dreamtime Dreamwheel, a *bonus* you received with this book!

Chapter Seven: Your DreamSelf Is the North Star Within . . . *True, Unchanging, a "Guide"* —Your Dreamtime Wrap-Up and Graduation

★ In Chapter Seven, the final chapter of the Dreamtime Dream Interpretation Book, I'll wrap up the Dreamtime Method and teach you how to use your *Magic Wand Within, the Triangle (Within You) for Transforming*. The *Triangle for Transforming* is a powerful, multi-dimensional technique/tool for wholeness that after learning and mastering the Dreamtime Method, you've earned! You won't want to miss reading this chapter!

Table of Contents

CHAPTER ONE

The Magician, Your DreamSelf Within

What if I told you someone is privately available to you who is free of charge and can solve—and I mean solve—any and all problems in your life, immediately. I will describe this person as being like a *Magician,* an energy that can wave a magic wand and give you the most valuable information with which you can resolve, for example, the problem of why you worry all the time. Or why no matter how hard you work, you never have enough money. Or why you are working at a job that pays you well, but doesn't really satisfy you creatively. Or why you are overweight or are starving yourself to stay thin. Or why you are drug- and/or alcohol-addicted. Or why you find yourself angry most of the time. Or why you feel stuck or lonely sometimes. Or why you may be in an abusive or dead-end relationship and are always afraid to make a change. Or why you sometimes feel empty and worthless, as though you don't deserve anything better in your life. And even if you did deserve better, why you still wouldn't know the first thing of how to go about changing it. Or finally, why, in your life right now, you aren't verbalizing your needs to yourself or others, but just keep accepting things as they are.

What if I told you that all of this doesn't matter and it's not too late for you… that this *Magician* can give you the *information* you need to solve, change, and create whatever you want, right in the here and now, to make you healthier and happier, immediately! Do you think that would be a valuable person to get to know? If you said, "Yes," and I'm sure you would, I will now introduce you to your own *DreamSelf Within,* who lives in the *Dreamtime* that's located *within you.*

We all want someone to tell us what to do to solve the problems in our lives. We want someone to tell us what to do to solve our troubles, and then we want *that someone to do it for us.* If I can be really honest here, deep within, this is how most of us have felt at one time or another in our lives. What a hassle it is making the right changes and doing all the hard stuff that we need to do to make things better for ourselves. It would be so much easier and less painful to let someone else do it for us. *Wouldn't it?*

Well, that person is available… right here and now. That person is deep within you, in your inner heart, your *DreamSelf Within,* the one who creates your dreams for you. By

1

taking the time to consciously learn what your dreams mean, you are connecting to the part of yourself within who not only has all the answers you need to create the situations you want in your life, but who also provides *the actual way* for you to do it! Read on to learn more...

About the Dreamtime Method

Hi, I'm the author of this book and I'm just like you. Admittedly, I've had my own share of major league problems in my life. In addition, I've been fascinated by my dreams, and you probably bought this book because of a similar fascination. In learning to interpret my dreams and then to connect that information and guidance to my everyday life, I opened up a huge door of new possibilities within myself. A door so large that to give you an example of the kind of knowledge you can glean from within, I got most of the information—the information you are going to learn as you read this book—through my dreams!

About nineteen years ago, I woke up one day and all of a sudden wanted to know what my dreams meant. So I took a workshop on dream interpretation. The workshop provided me with several popular dream interpretation dictionaries with which to look up the meanings of my dream symbols. The idea was that the dream dictionaries were to assist me in interpreting and understanding what my dreams meant. So I wrote my dreams down faithfully, and then used the dream dictionaries to interpret them. But after using the dream dictionaries for a period of time, I realized all too clearly that a dream dictionary was perhaps someone else's idea of what a dream symbol should mean and *not necessarily mine.*

Determined and excited to learn what my dreams were telling me, I continued to write my dreams down and to use the dream dictionaries to interpret them. Then after doing this for a while, something happened. I began to sense a distinct *"view"* of how my dream symbols were being communicated to me in my dreams. Whoever was giving me my dreams used common, everyday symbols that we all see in our dreams. But what I began to grasp as unique was the *perspective* of where these meanings were coming from and how they were being given to me. I will describe this perspective as one of coming from *a much larger and expansive view* than what we are all used to experiencing in our everyday, physical lives. The vantage point of where my dream symbols were being given to me from the dream state was definitely *wider, less limited, and more encompassing* than the usual three-dimensional view that we see and feel in our physical world.

For a long time, I thought about this much "larger perspective" that was being communicated to me from my dreams. Then one day, as I was interpreting my dreams, a light came on! I said to myself: Whoever is giving me my dreams, I know how they are doing it! That's when I began to figure out how to use the "larger perspective" as *a way of thinking* to accurately interpret my dreams. Putting aside the dream dictionaries, I began to understand that as I used this *"expanded perspective,"* I was intuiting as a *method of thinking* that I could then use it to figure out what my dream symbols were saying to me on my own and what they accurately meant!

What I discovered as I accurately interpreted my own dreams was that I began to *"think"* just like the part of myself within who was giving me my dreams. I knew I was on to something then… because now whenever I used my simple dream interpretation method to interpret my dreams, it invariably *reflected exact guidance and information* that was "dead on" accurate *for what was going on within my life.* As I used this "unique way of thinking" to interpret my dreams, I found—just as you will as you read this book—that I essentially *became* my own dream dictionary. I did not need to rely on anything *outside of myself*, whether a dream dictionary or anyone else, to accurately interpret and understand what my dreams meant.

And my easy-to-do method worked reliably every time I used it!

I continued using my Dreamtime Method to interpret my dreams with great accuracy for years. Eventually I found myself wondering if my method for understanding dreams may also be reliable in interpreting dreams for others. Being inquisitive, sixteen years ago I created a website on the Internet, www.dreaminterpretation.com, to test my dream methodology for accuracy.

I asked people to record their dreams via e-mail; then, at no charge, I'd interpret the dreams using the Dreamtime Method. I would then e-mail an interpretation back, asking for a response about whether it related to their life or not.

Well, the results I got back were astounding! I got reports back from all over the world about the dreams I'd interpreted using my simple Dreamtime Method. Invariably the respondents were people I did not know and about whom I knew nothing, yet these individuals e-mailed me back with amazing testimonials saying that what I had interpreted for them matched exactly what was going on in their lives! They were amazed at the guidance and information I was able to provide about their lives *just from a dream*!

Dreamtime Method Overview

Here's an overview of what you are about to learn. The Dreamtime Method is an easy-to-do, logical, step-by-step process where you learn to *think of your dream symbols* just as your DreamSelf Within does, the *multi-dimensional energy from within you* that creates your dreams. Learning to "think" of your dream symbols as your DreamSelf Within does gives you an absolutely accurate interpretation of your dream. This is because you are getting the interpretation from the horse's mouth, so to say! You understand your dreams the same way as your DreamSelf Within who creates them.

In sharing my story of how I learned to interpret my dreams using my Dreamtime Method as *a way of thinking*, it created a vast opening of consciousness within me. The reason that this will also happen for you is because once you learn to interpret your dream symbols consciously and to connect the information and guidance to your everyday life, the awareness you attain within *unlimits you!* As you interpret your dreams and bring into your everyday Self and life the unlimited consciousness of your DreamSelf Within, you transform into *that expanded awareness and become it* right here in the third dimension!

As you open your inner dream door, you become *the alchemist and the conscious creator of your three-dimensional life.* Thus you take what seems ordinary in your everyday life and understand it as something *extraordinary.* As you interpret your dreams consciously and connect their guidance to your daily life, you stop looking at yourself and your life only through the three dimensional keyhole of your current, waking reality. You open your *multi-dimensional dream door* which makes available to you the wealth of unlimited knowledge and information that is you and your DreamSelf Within.

But just how do you start on this exciting journey of interpreting your dreams *consciously* as you travel from your *inside-out?* You begin at the beginning! That means, beginning with the first step of the Dreamtime Method. Understanding the foundation of which we are all made, which is *multi-dimensional energy.*

CHAPTER TWO

The Foundation for Interpreting Your Dreams Accurately: Understanding Yourself as a Multi-Dimensional Energy Being

"Mirror, mirror on the wall . . .
Who's the deepest of them all?
You are!"

You and everything on this earth and in our galaxy are made up of energy. You and I are *magnetic* Energy Beings.

As I teach you to learn how to interpret your dreams, you may be wondering why I begin with a discussion of what energy is and how it works. I start with the importance of understanding what energy is and how it functions because your dream energy that you dream every night is creating the *three dimensional energy* you recognize as you, your physical Self, and your Life! Your dream energy that you dream through the Universal *Law of Attraction* creates and draws in similar energy to you—creating what you now know as you, your physical Self and Life.

Energy

Let's look now at what the definition of "energy" is:

• Energy is best defined as *vibration*.

Energy works, operates, and creates through a Universal Law, the Law of Attraction. This Law states that a *like energy* vibration attracts a similar or like energy vibration. Simply put, *like attracts like*. We have all heard the old saying, "Birds of a feather flock together." It's no mistake that energy creates and is attracted to similar energy, since energy naturally flows that way through Universal Law.

5

Further defining energy as vibration . . . you should know that vibration can and *does* exist at varied rates of frequency. To show how energy can and does exist at varied rates of vibrational frequency in our three-dimensional world, let's use the simple example of water. As it pours out of our taps, water exists as energy at a rate of vibrational frequency that we, in the third dimension, consider to be *physical or solid*. This is illustrated for you in *figure 2.1*. When water exists in this physical state, it is at a slow rate of vibrational frequency. When water is in its slowed-down rate of vibrational frequency, it is considered solid and something that we can visibly see with our naked eye.

When you take that very same water and increase its rate of vibrational frequency by boiling it, it turns into steam. This is illustrated in *figure 2.2*.

Water, when it exists as steam, is at a much faster rate of vibrational frequency than when it is in its slowed down physical and solid state. The steam version of water evaporates into the air and eventually becomes what we in the third dimension consider to be non-physical or invisible. We think of this as being invisible to the naked eye because we can't see it, yet we know that it's still there and consider it to be a version of water.

In my workshops as we are talking about energy, it is at this point that I ask everyone to pull their dream energy out and put it down in front of them. I ask each one of my workshop participants to take their dream energy out, not what they wrote down from their dreams, but *their actual dream energy*, so that we can all get an idea what dreams look like in the physical world and see them. Everyone sits puzzled for a short time and then they begin to laugh. *What a trick question!*

They all begin to realize that they can't pull their actual dream energy out because their dream energy is not anything that is physical. But everyone knows they have dreams and that they are something; otherwise they wouldn't be attending a workshop or buying this book to learn to interpret them!

Your dream energy exists non-physically, yet you know it is real. This is because you, as a total Energy Being, exist at many frequencies of vibration within, much like the water does. What you recognize as your physical body and Self in the material world is actually your inner energy existing at a slowed down rate of vibration, perceived by you in the third dimension as physical and solid. What you are recognizing as your *dream energy*, as non-physical or invisible, is your inner energy existing at a very high rate of vibration.

You as an Energy Being

Now look on page 9 at *figure 2.3* labeled "You As An 'Energy Being.'" In this illustration, imagine that the figure in the picture is you looking at yourself as total energy.

Just beyond the outer, dark outline of the figure, imagine yourself existing at a very high or fast rate of vibrational frequency. This outer form represents you and your dream energy within where you perceive it in the third dimension as being non-physical or invisible.

Figure 2.1

Figure 2.2

Now look at the area inside the outline of the form in *figure 2.3*.

I want you to imagine that this is your faster vibrating, non-physical energy (the energy outside the form in the picture) that is now *slowing down* in vibration where it then becomes *physical* and *visible* in the third-dimension. The area inside the form is you and your higher vibrating, non-physical energy in a slowed down state of vibration which then creates, becomes and is the energy of the physical, three-dimensional world. The illustration in *figure 2.3* says that the area inside the outline of the form is your energy existing at slow rate of vibration which is being perceived by you (in the everyday, physical world) as your three-dimensional Self and life.

To further define the visualization that I just gave you of yourself as energy, I now want you to look at *figure 2.4*: "Multi-Dimensional' DreamSelf As A Total And Whole Energy Being." *Figure 2.4* is a *side-look* view of *figure 2.3* that was just illustrated.

In *figure 2.4*, as you look at the left side of this picture, starting with what is labeled the 10th dimension (10-D), I want you to imagine that this is the center of your non-physical energy Self within. This is your energy where it is being perceived as invisible and is vibrating at a very high and fast rate of vibrational frequency.

Now as you look from left to right in *figure 2.4*, as your non-physical energy slows down in vibration, it extends from the 10th dimension (10-D) through all the other dimensions (9, 8, 7, 6, 5, and 4D) of yourself within, where it then becomes visible or what you are now perceiving as the physical 3rd dimension, (you, your physical Self and life). The 3rd dimension in this illustration is your inner energy at a slowed down rate of vibrational frequency and, as noted above, is what you are now recognizing as the physical "you" of your everyday life.

The non-physical (or invisible) part of you within that exists from the 4th through the 10th dimension in *figure 2.4* is what I now want you to know and understand as your inner Self, your Divine Self, your *DreamSelf Within*. This is the part of you that creates your non-physical dreams and your subsequent created physical, three-dimensional Self and life. All of the "non-physical dimensions" of yourself within are what I call and refer to as The Dreamtime.

➳ The Dreamtime, then, is the faster-vibrating, non-physical dimensions of your energy, which is also your *DreamSelf Within*.

Visualizing and thinking about yourself as noted above, begins to demonstrate to you how you may now start to perceive yourself as a *multi-dimensional Energy Being* or as a "Being" of many dimensions within. Looking at yourself in this expanded way allows you to understand that you are not just a Being who exists *only* in the physical 3rd dimension. This illustration shows how you may now think and understand yourself as a Being who lives in many dimensions of vibrational energy within (which you do)!

Figure 2.3

You As An "Energy Being"

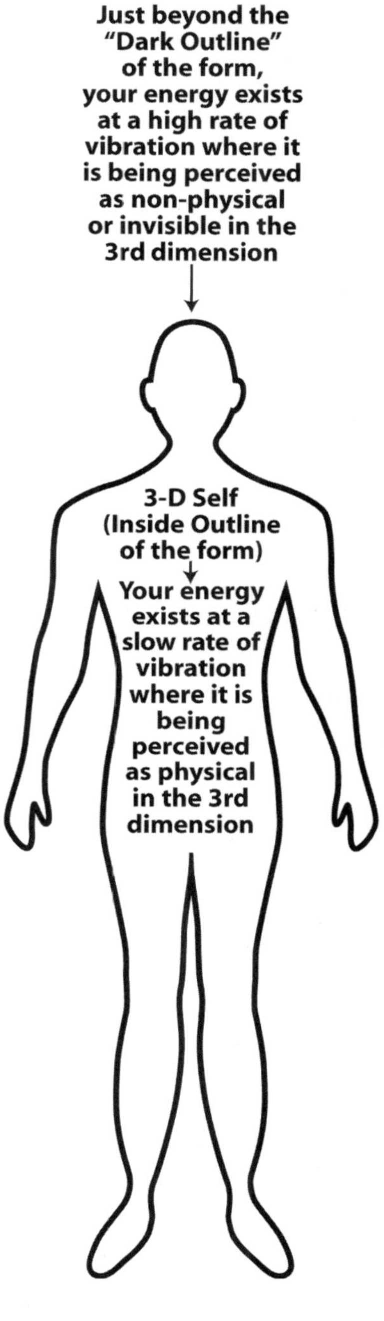

Just beyond the
"Dark Outline"
of the form,
your energy exists
at a high rate of
vibration where it
is being perceived
as non-physical
or invisible in the
3rd dimension

↓

3-D Self
(Inside Outline
of the form)
↓
Your energy
exists at a
slow rate of
vibration
where it is
being
perceived
as physical
in the 3rd
dimension

Figure 2.4

"Multi-Dimensional" DreamSelf As A Total and Whole Energy Being

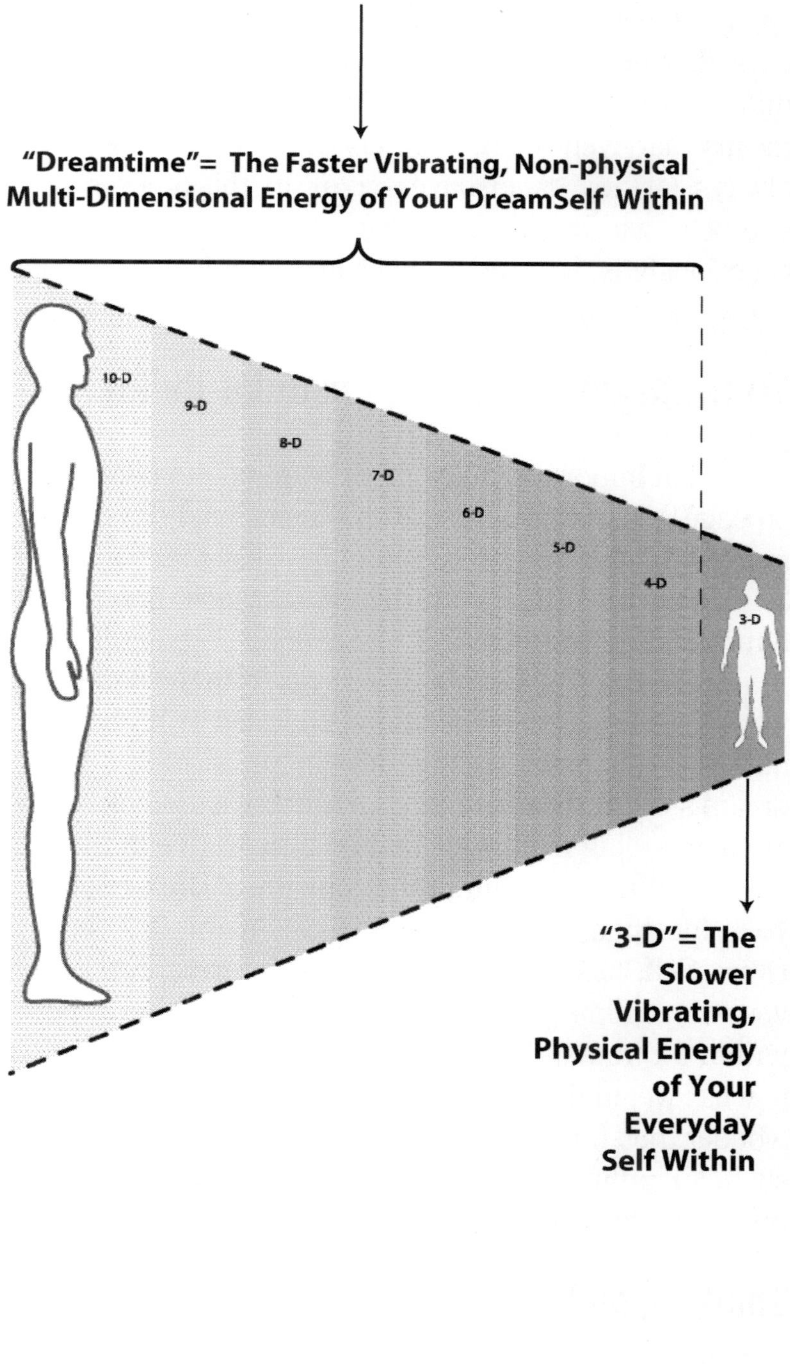

↓

"Dreamtime"= The Faster Vibrating, Non-physical
Multi-Dimensional Energy of Your DreamSelf Within

10-D   9-D   8-D   7-D   6-D   5-D   4-D   3-D

"3-D"= The
Slower
Vibrating,
Physical Energy
of Your
Everyday
Self Within

As you begin to think and conceptualize yourself as a Being of many dimensions of energy within (as described in *figures 2.3 & 2.4*), it is important to understand that all of the non-physical and physical dimensions of yourself are always vibrating together in concert and at once! To clarify this thought further, think of the energies of your non-physical and physical Self existing as *corresponding* dimensions of energy together. Your energy dimensions vibrate faster to slower, but always *simultaneously*. This understanding says that even though the many dimensions of your energy Self may be vibrating at different rates of energy frequency, you, as a total energy Being, always exist *as one*. This means that even though you are awake in the 3rd dimension and living out your day, you always (at any time) have access to the other *simultaneously vibrating dimensions* of yourself within. In fact, your desire now to understand what your dreams mean consciously is, in multi-dimensional reality, your inner DreamSelf's wish for you to get to know and recognize your *non-physical Self* within!

Your Larger Multi-Dimensional Picture Within

An important point that I want you to take note of, while looking back at *figure 2.4* on page 9, is that, from the 10th dimension, I have illustrated your energy existing at a far more expanded perspective than the view that you now have of yourself from the physical 3rd dimension. This is illustrated in *figure 2.4* by the cut-lines tapering from the 10th dimension down to the 3rd.

The reason for this is because, from the non-physical dimensions of yourself within, where your energy exists at an expanded or high rate of vibration, your consciousness is not limited to experiencing only the physical 3rd dimension. The view you have from the dream state and Dreamtime is a much vaster look of yourself and your life than what you are now seeing from your limited perspective in the 3rd dimension.

In understanding that your inner DreamSelf has a much larger view of you and your life than what you now have in the 3rd dimension, this means that your inner DreamSelf has access to *unlimited* information, knowledge, and resources for you and your three-dimensional life. This unlimited information that your DreamSelf possesses within for you and your life is of an *extremely powerful and extraordinary intelligence*. It is what we, in the 3rd dimension, might consider as being All-Knowing or Divine. Is it no wonder then that your dreams have such great guidance for you and your life coming from such an unlimited part of yourself within? And the best thing about learning and understanding all of this, is that this extraordinary resource is located right inside of you!

Thinking Multi-Dimensionally

As mentioned earlier, the Dreamtime Method of interpretation is learning how to think as your DreamSelf Within, the part of you that creates your dreams.

⇒ Learning to "think"—as your DreamSelf Within—gives you an absolutely accurate interpretation of your dreams. The reason why is that you are thinking *just as the part of yourself within* that creates your dreams.

If you were not able to first perceive yourself as being "multi-dimensional energy" as demonstrated for you in the previous illustrations, how could you ever accurately figure out the perspective that this part of yourself within has as it creates your dreams for you? You really couldn't. Not knowing how to think *multi-dimensionally* and then trying to interpret your multi-dimensional dreams accurately would be like me saying to myself: Today I am going out to repair my car engine, although I don't know the first thing about car repair nor do I know how an engine operates!

When interpreting your dreams, if you did not view yourself the way your DreamSelf Within does as it creates your dreams and dream symbols for you, you would get, at best, the popular, but *limited* psychological interpretation of your dreams. Getting a purely psychological interpretation of your dreams means that the information your dream symbols are communicating would be limited in their meaning/understanding to only that of the 3rd dimension. It would also mean that your dreams and dream symbols *true* multi-dimensional meaning for you and your life would be obscure and remain shrouded in the unknown.

With the Dreamtime Method of interpreting your dreams, you are learning first where your dreams originate, multi-dimensionally from within you. And, about your inner DreamSelf's unique, powerful and unlimited perspective, as just visualized in *figures 2.3 and 2.4.*

Your 3rd Dimensional versus 10th Dimensional Perspective Within

In telling you that a multi-dimensional perspective is the way that your dream symbols are being communicated to you in your dreams, the most logical way to continue to understand this expanded perspective of yourself within is to begin with a dimensional view we are all familiar with. That is your current three dimensional view of the physical world.

I'd like you now to turn to page 12 and look at *figure 2.5.* This graphic shows a person standing on Earth with the sun, sky, and stars above their head. I think we would all agree that this is the usual way we view the physical world from our third-dimensional *perspective*. We all view the sun, sky, and stars from the third dimension as being *outside* of our physical body and Self.

Now look at *figure 2.6* on page 13, labeled: "Your Multi-Dimensional DreamSelf's 10th Dimensional 'Consciousness' with Its Thinking, View And Perspective of You And The Physical Third Dimension." *Figure 2.6* illustrates how your DreamSelf

Figure 2.5

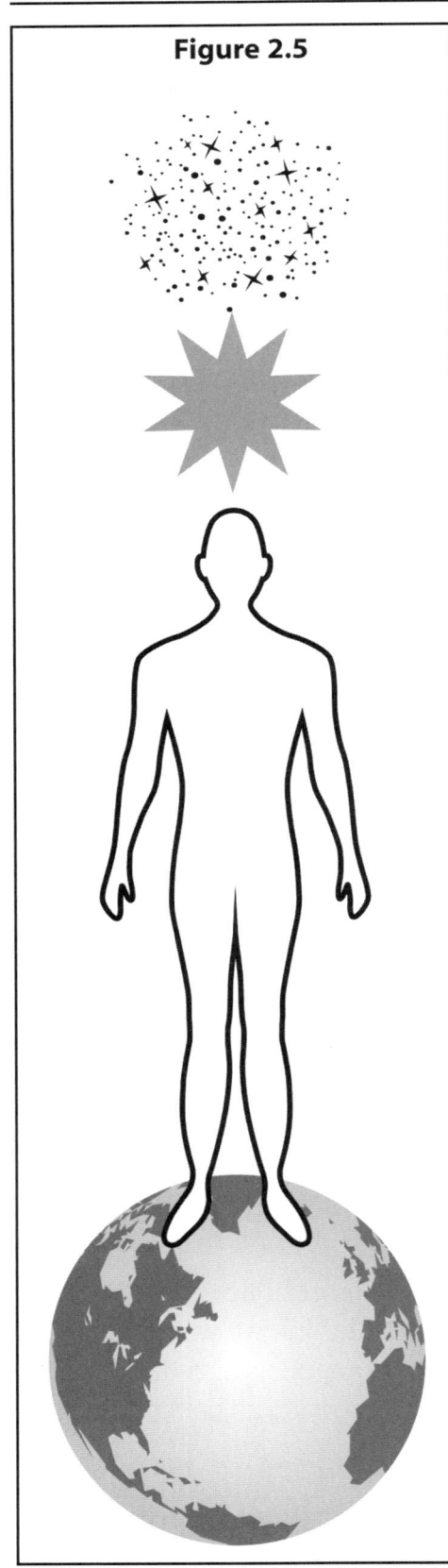

views you and your three dimensional life from its 10th dimensional perspective. It then illustrates how from that 10th dimensional perspective, it goes on to *think* as it creates your dream symbols for you in your dreams.

As you have learned from our previous illustrations, as you and your DreamSelf's 10th dimensional energy slows in vibration, it becomes what you are recognizing as the physical third dimension. This means that all of the physical third dimension is then a *slowed down version* of the faster vibrating, non-physical energy of the 10th dimension, which is your non-physical Self, your DreamSelf Within.

In understanding this, as your DreamSelf creates your dream symbols for you, its method of communicating to you, its three-dimensional Self, is to look at each dream symbol as though it were an actual aspect of physical energy originating from within both of you. Your DreamSelf looks at all energy of the physical world as parts or aspects of your and its own energy because the third dimension is the slower vibrating energy of your faster vibrating 10th dimensional Self.

This means that your DreamSelf looks at all energy of the third dimension, which includes your dream symbols, as though they are all then *physical aspects and abilities* of energy originating from the core energy of you (and its) 10th dimensional energy from within. As you can see illustrated in *figure 2.6,* from your DreamSelf's multi-dimensional perspective, you, your life, and everything it creates in the third dimension is viewed and perceived as its own "slowed down physical energy" that comes from the "faster moving non-physical energy" of you and itself within.

Understanding Your Inner Multi-Dimensional/Three-Dimensional Mirror

Now turn to *figure 2.7* on page 15. *Figure 2.7* takes the understanding of *figure 2.6* and illustrates the multi-dimensional perspective that your DreamSelf

Figure 2.6

Your Multi-Dimensional DreamSelf's 10th Dimensional 'Consciousness' With Its Thinking, View And Perspective of You And The Physical Third Dimension

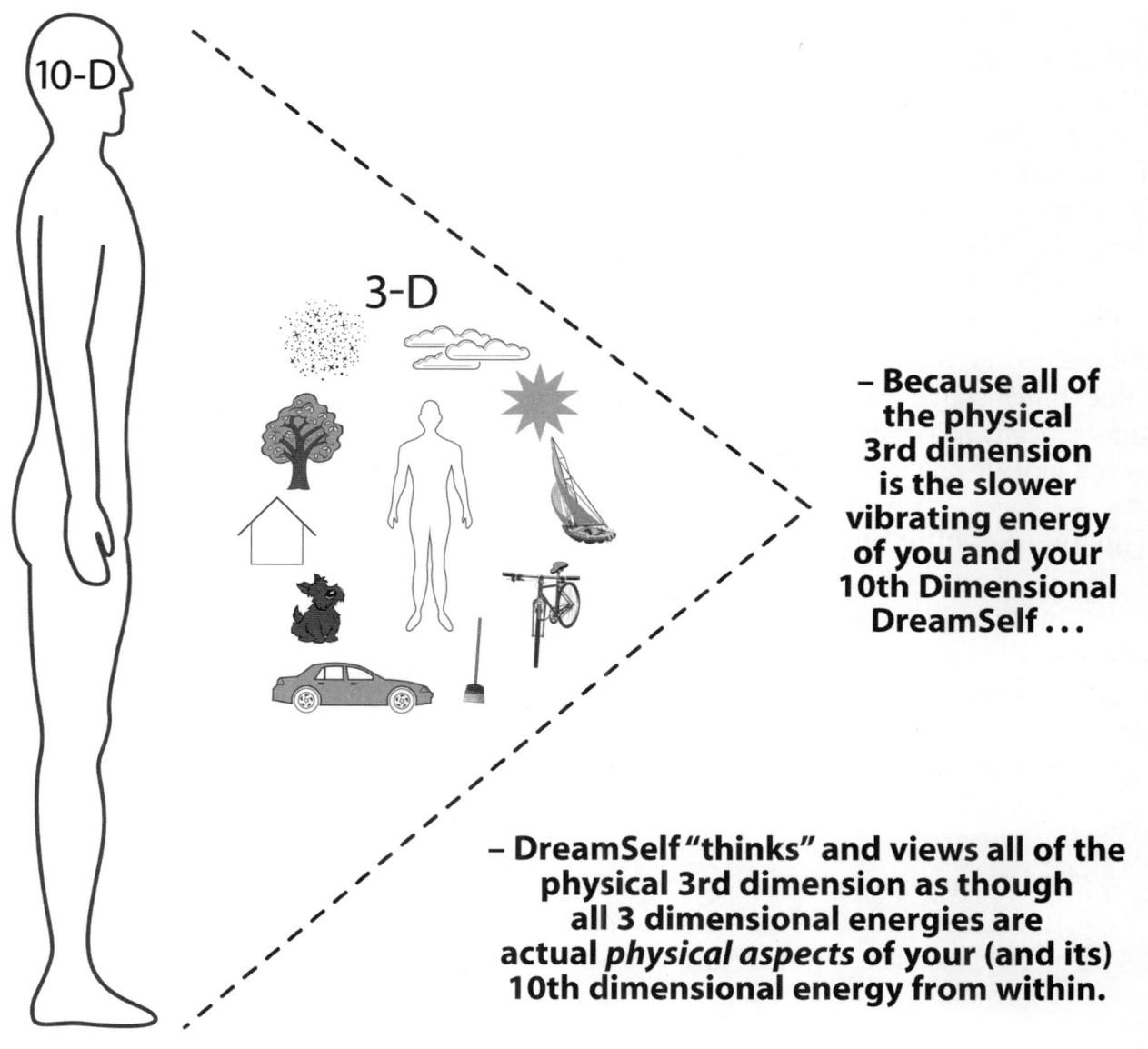

10-D

3-D

– Because all of the physical 3rd dimension is the slower vibrating energy of you and your 10th Dimensional DreamSelf . . .

– DreamSelf "thinks" and views all of the physical 3rd dimension as though all 3 dimensional energies are actual *physical aspects* of your (and its) 10th dimensional energy from within.

Your DreamSelf *thinks* in this way because multi-dimensionally . . . they are!

has of the third dimension more deeply. In this illustration, I have your DreamSelf looking into a mirror. Now instead of your DreamSelf seeing its own reflection being shown back from the mirror that it is looking into, what is being shown is all energy of the third dimension which includes you, your physical Self, and your life.

This deeper perspective from your DreamSelf means that everything you now view in the third dimension as being physically separate from yourself in your everyday world is really a *mirror image* of the non-physical, faster vibrating 10th dimensional energies of you and your DreamSelf Within. Because the third dimension is the slower vibrating energy of your 10th dimensional Self, when I say that your DreamSelf communicates each of your dream symbols as though they are *actual physical aspects and abilities* of the energy of you and itself, your DreamSelf does this because, multi-dimensionally, they are! This also means that everything in your everyday, outer physical world is then *an aspect of yourself* within as it accordingly reflects your inner Self, your total and whole multi-dimensional DreamSelf Within.

Seeing your DreamSelf's multi-dimensional perspective illustrated and explained in this way, you can see why your DreamSelf communicates and uses everyday "physical objects and events" as your dream symbols. It does this because it knows that you, its three dimensional Self, are most understanding of the physical world and will automatically associate a *physical meaning* with what it is trying to say and communicate to you in your dreams with your dream symbols.

The Two Specific Functions of Your Dreams and Dream Symbols

In stating that your dreams are a multi-dimensional energy that your DreamSelf also perceives as being your and its *physical, three dimensional energy*, your dream symbols perform two specific functions in your everyday, physical life:

#1. Your dreams and dream symbols, as energy, are a communication from your DreamSelf that *tell* you exactly what's going on in your everyday life.

#2. Your non-physical dream energy as it slows down and becomes physical, three dimensional energy, also *creates*. Your dream energy *creates* in the third dimension by attracting into you and your next day, after dreaming your dream, more and similar *physical energy* to accomplish and manifest (make happen) whatever your dream is addressing. It is in this way that your dreams as *energy* create your everyday physical Self and life!

When I first began interpreting other people's dreams for them, I could tell, from interpreting their dreams, that these individuals were somehow being impulsed and

Figure 2.7

Your DreamSelf perceiving all of the Physical Third Dimension as Its own *slower* vibrating 10th Dimensional Energy, so therefore all of the Third Dimension is Its Reflection and "Mirror-Image"

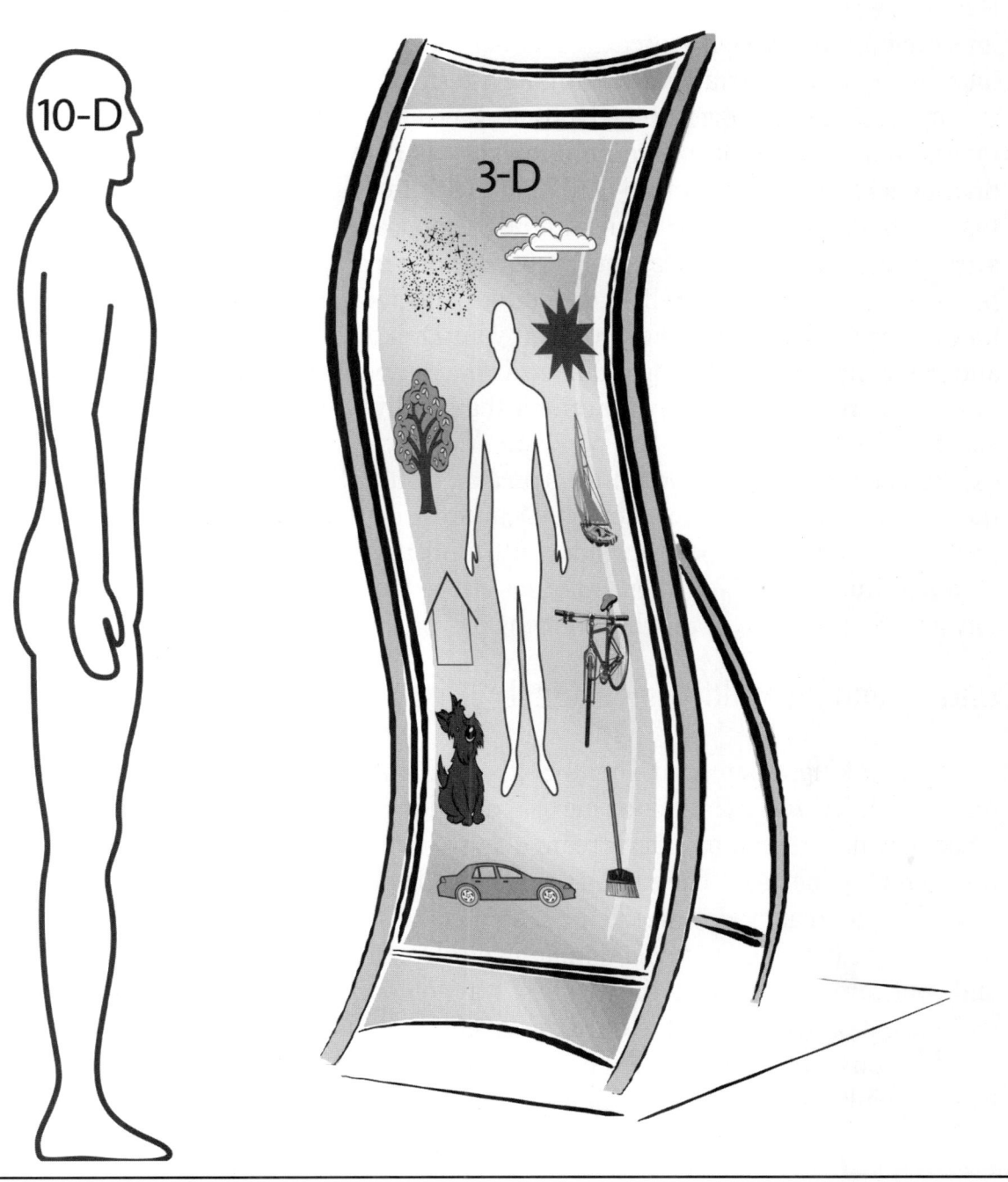

triggered into action in their waking life by their dream symbols after they had dreamed them. Here's what I mean by this… you know how you can have a dream where you may be having an argument with someone and then you wake up feeling angry? Or maybe you've had a pleasant dream and then wake up feeling happy and at peace?

I knew that after dreaming our dream symbols, we were somehow being affected by them and that this then went on into our physical day to correspond to emotion and action. Since most people do not interpret their dreams consciously, I knew that they had to be getting the benefit of their dreams somehow, *whether they understood them or not.* But how was this happening? I wondered about this for years. As time went on and as I interpreted other people's dreams for them, they would often tell me, "What you have interpreted for me is exactly what is going on in my life!" Finally, over the years, I put these two understandings together and a light came on. The reason the dream interpretations I interpreted for other people captured what was going on in their lives was because their dreams, as energy, were actively creating their three-dimensional lives! I learned, as noted, that your dreams as your own multi-dimensional/three dimensional energy create by attracting in similar physical energy, which then manifests what you know as *the energy* that is you, your physical Self, and your life. This means that your dreams as the conscious thoughts (magnetic energy) of you and your DreamSelf are creating and drawing to you and your physical life the three dimensional energy of whatever you are dreaming about.

We in the third dimension think that we live out our physical day and then go to sleep and dream. It's just the opposite! You non-physically dream first and then you experience the physical third dimension as a result! Now when speaking to people about their dreams, I explain their non-physical dream energy comes first! Your dream energy (your faster vibrating non-physical 10th dimensional DreamSelf Within) creates your dream symbols, and you then *wake up* to the slower vibrating energy of your *created* physical Self and life in the third dimension.

Understanding Multi-Dimensional "Time" Within

Thinking about your DreamSelf's *unlimited perspective* as illustrated for you in *figures 2.4, 2.6 and 2.7,* reminds me of a question people often ask me. They want to know when they have a dream, is that dream relevant to today or is the dream referring to another time possibly the past? They also ask me how long do the effects of a dream stay with you? If you had a dream today, would it be referring to something in the next few days or to the future? Now that you are understanding your DreamSelf's "panoramic perspective" of you and your three-dimensional life, the best way to answer those questions is to take a look at the concept of what we in the third dimension know and call *time.*

In our solid, physical third dimension, we count time as *linear* or in a successive way of thinking and understanding. We have yesterday or the past. We have now or today.

And then we have tomorrow or what we consider to be our future. Because the third dimension is the extended, slower vibrating energy of your 10th dimensional Self (illustrated in *figure 2.4* back on page 9), your DreamSelf looks at time in the third dimension as being *non-linear* or as having no time line. That means from your DreamSelf's multi-dimensional perspective, regarding how it communicates your dreams to you, time is thought of as existing only in the *now*.

When we speak, in the third dimension, of a past experience, we think of something that has occurred previously or that is not part of our present experience. From your multi-dimensional DreamSelf's perspective, because the third dimension is the slower vibrating energy of your (and its) non-linear 10th dimensional energy, a *past* experience that you may have had in the third dimension is not considered as something that is separate or apart from you now. From your DreamSelf's perspective, because it possesses such a large multi-dimensional view of yourself as illustrated in *figures 2.6* and *2.7* on pages 13 and 15, it does not consider an experience you may have had in the past as being separate, but rather as being the sum total of the whole multi-dimensional *you* that you are now.

Thinking non-linearly, or as though everything that ever was is existing in your now, your DreamSelf looks at you as though you are the past or as though you are now the culmination of what you may have been or done in the past. An example would be that all of the talents and abilities that you have garnered in any past life or experience, your DreamSelf Within knows that they all exist and are here *within you now*.

In speaking of the future, from our third-dimensional perspective, the *future* is the thought of an *intention to create* or do something at another given time. But from your multi-dimensional DreamSelf's non-linear way of thinking, "intention" is what is creating your now in the present moment. How this can be understood is that from your inner DreamSelf's way of thinking through Universal Law, your magnetic energy of thought is what is creating and attracting your present everyday three dimensional life right here in the moment! In saying this, from your DreamSelf's view, what you are currently thinking is what is creating your now... in the now! This means that your three-dimensional intention to create (a.k.a. the future) is what is, in multi-dimensional reality, creating your present everyday physical reality instantly!

In understanding your multi-dimensional DreamSelf's non-linear way of thinking, my answer regarding the effect of people's dreams on themselves and their lives is that your dream energy through the Law of Attraction *is* creating your three-dimensional reality, your now, so your dream's content is what in our physical world is the past, the present, and the future! This also means that because your dreams are a non-linear, multi-dimensional energy, you, your dream energy, and DreamSelf are eternal with no beginning or end! Thus as you use the Dreamtime Method and interpret your dreams, you internalize your dream energy *consciously* and begin to live your life as your DreamSelf Within does, which is in the present moment. You will be living only in the "now."

The Origin of Your DreamSelf Within

Now that you understand the larger perspective of your DreamSelf Within, the next step of the Dreamtime Method is to understand exactly where (from within you) your expanded, unlimited multi-dimensional dream energy originates and comes from. Why? By understanding the non-physical dimensions of where you and your DreamSelf originate, you learn more about the creative energy and power of your whole multi-dimensional Self that lies within!

Learning more about your multi-dimensional Self within allows you to expand the concept of who you may think you are now to then transform *the you* of your current, everyday three dimensional Self and your life. And in learning that your dreams and DreamSelf are a multi-dimensional energy that creates your three-dimensional Self and life, as you interpret your dreams and understand what they mean, I guarantee that you will begin to wonder, just as I did, exactly where from within you your *extraordinary dream energy* comes from! As you interpret your dreams and consciously understand what these dreams mean, you'll begin to think deeper and deeper about yourself, your dreams, and your dream energy.

With this understanding, how do you move forward to find out what kind of energy you and your dreams are made of? Well, you move forward by doing what you have learned to do so far in this book, which is to *think* multi-dimensionally just as your DreamSelf Within does!

You Thinking Multi-Dimensionally

To do this, let's start with the multi-dimensional understanding you've just learned . . . our physical third dimension is the slower vibrating energy of you and your 10th dimensional DreamSelf that lies within. This understanding puts forth the idea that if all of the third dimension is the "mirror image" energy of you and your 10th dimensional DreamSelf . . . then the energy in our physical world that you view as being *farthest away* from your vision in the 3rd dimension has to be and is then closest to your DreamSelf's 10th dimensional faster-vibrating *core energy within*.

The farthest physical elements of energy that one can see from the third dimension, elements that appear to be outside of our Self in the physical world, are the stars, the sky and our sun. Taking the cosmic energy of the stars, the sky, and of the sun, and thinking multi-dimensionally, now look at *figure 2.8* on page 19: "Your Dream Energy."

Since the Milky Way Galaxy of stars is the farthest energy that you can physically see from the 3rd dimension, when you think multi-dimensionally, this creates the understanding that your non-physical DreamSelf's 10th dimensional core energy originates as *nuclear star energy*.

Let me explain this further. The stars of our Milky Way Galaxy are the farthest

18

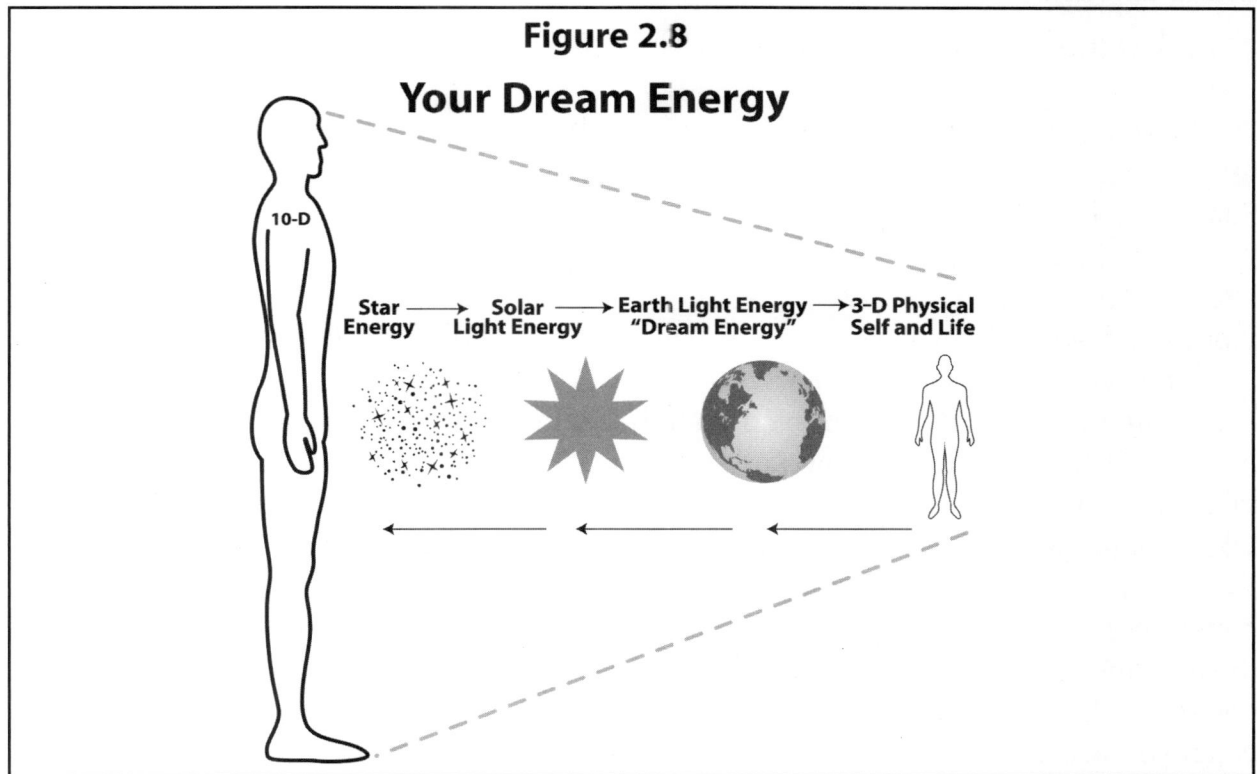

Figure 2.8

Your Dream Energy

10-D

Star Energy → Solar Light Energy → Earth Light Energy "Dream Energy" → 3-D Physical Self and Life

energy one can visualize as being away from their physical view in the third-dimension. Because our third dimension is the slower vibrating energy of our 10th dimensional DreamSelf that lies within, the furthest energy you can visualize from the 3rd dimension is the closest to our DreamSelf's core energy. Thinking in this multi-dimensional way, this postulates that your DreamSelf and dreams must then originate as *nuclear star energy vibration.*

Remember earlier when I said that all energy is governed by the Universal Law of Attraction, the rule that like energy attracts like energy? Your dreams, as energy, are *directed* in exactly the same way! As your DreamSelf and dream energy originate as nuclear star energy, they are then attracted to the next similar energy on their spiraling pathway of energy vibration towards Earth.

The next closest similar energy from the nuclear star energy of the Milky Way Galaxy on its pathway of vibration towards Earth is the nuclear solar energy of the Sun. To get a clearer picture of this thought, look again now at *figure 2.8*. This figure illustrates for you how the nuclear star energy of the Milky Way Galaxy, as it spirals out vibrating on its energy pathway, then connects to the Sun as solar energy.

Now we all understand how solar energy radiates to the Earth as light energy vibration. Putting all of the above cosmic energy connections together, this understanding means that what you are perceiving as your dreams in the third dimension originates within you as nuclear star energy vibration. As the star energy vibration (that is your dreams) spirals on its pathway, it then connects as energy vibration to the energy of our Sun. The Sun's solar light energy vibration then radiates to Earth and that energy, in multi-dimensional reality, is what you are perceiving in the third dimension as *your dreams.*

Your DreamSelf as a Complete and Eternal System Within

To further illustrate where from within you your dream energy originates, turn now to *figure 2.9:* "Your Multi-Dimensional DreamSelf As A Complete System Eternally Sustaining Itself" on page 21.

Starting with the head of the figure, this illustration shows how you and your DreamSelf's 10th dimensional energy and consciousness originate as nuclear star energy vibration from and beyond our Milky Way Galaxy band of stars. *Figure 2.9* illustrates how the *stellar light energy vibrations* that are your dreams may be visualized as the "thinking and thoughts" of you and your 10th dimensional DreamSelf that lies within. *Figure 2.9* then illustrates how you and your DreamSelf's thoughts (stellar/star light vibrations) transmit through the Universal Law of Attraction, spiraling as light energy vibration to the Sun.

What you are experiencing as your dreams in the third dimension are, in multi-dimensional reality, light energy vibrations from our Sun. The solar *light* which is your dreams, then enters the spiraling light encoded filaments of the DNA of your physical body and that is how you are getting the information that is being transmitted to you when you wake up remembering you had a dream. Your DreamSelf, through solar light energy vibration, communicates unlimited information—unlimited to you as its *inner thoughts*, which are your dreams.

The above understanding says that your dreams are then *light information transfers* of energy that are a communication of *information* from yourself in your non-physical, multi-dimensional form to yourself in your physical, three dimensional form. Your dream symbols are light energy vibrations that carry information from the faster vibrating 10th dimensional form of yourself within, to the slower vibrating energy of your physical Self that exists here in the third dimension. Understanding your dreams as solar light that is information, then means that solar light is a carrier and transmitter of information. Solar light multi-dimensionally is information. *Light is information!*

The Moon's Reflective Role in Our Dreams

When I say that our dreams are the conscious *thinking and thoughts* of information from our DreamSelf that come to us in the form of solar light, you may wonder how we physically get the solar light that is our dreams when the Sun isn't shining on us as we sleep at night?

We receive the solar light transmissions of information that are our dreams from our DreamSelf Within through the action of the *Moon.* I now want you to look again at *figure 2.9.* The Moon, a satellite of Earth, performs as a *screen-like filter* to all of the planets surrounding Earth, including our Sun. The Moon has no light of its own.

Figure 2.9

Your Multi-Dimensional DreamSelf As A Complete System Eternally Sustaining Itself

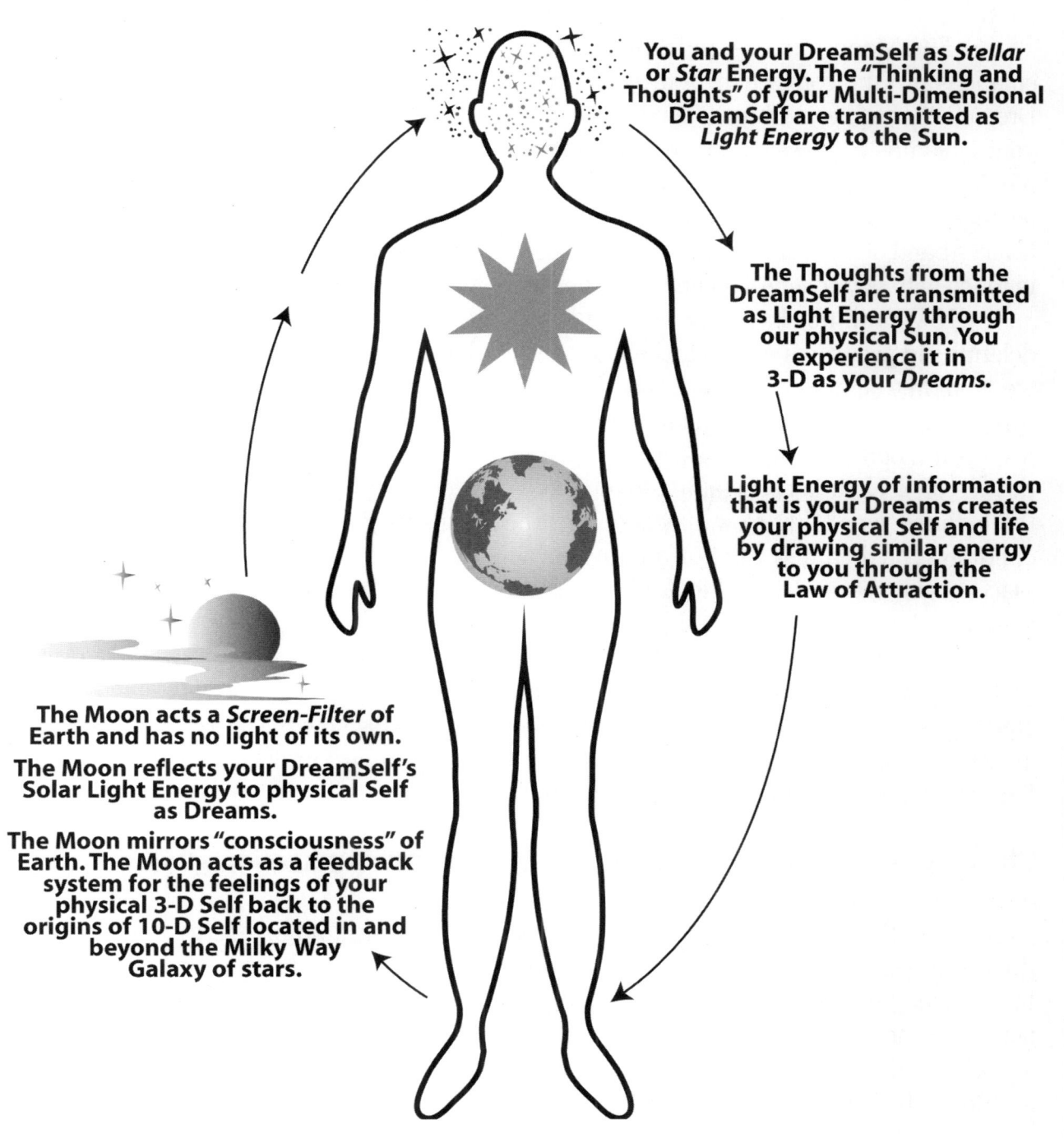

You and your DreamSelf as *Stellar* or *Star* Energy. The "Thinking and Thoughts" of your Multi-Dimensional DreamSelf are transmitted as *Light Energy* to the Sun.

The Thoughts from the DreamSelf are transmitted as Light Energy through our physical Sun. You experience it in 3-D as your *Dreams*.

Light Energy of information that is your Dreams creates your physical Self and life by drawing similar energy to you through the Law of Attraction.

The Moon acts a *Screen-Filter* of Earth and has no light of its own.

The Moon reflects your DreamSelf's Solar Light Energy to physical Self as Dreams.

The Moon mirrors "consciousness" of Earth. The Moon acts as a feedback system for the feelings of your physical 3-D Self back to the origins of 10-D Self located in and beyond the Milky Way Galaxy of stars.

The Moon reflects solar light energy from the Sun to the Earth and that is how (as illustrated for you in *figure 2.9* on page 21) while we sleep, we experience the sun's light energy of information as our dreams. When the Moon is full, it is completely lit by the Sun and that is why you have such intense dream experiences during a full Moon. When the Moon is full, you are getting the full light of your DreamSelf Within. This could be imagined as though a flashlight is being shined on you to get your conscious attention of what is going on within you and your life through your dreams.

The Moon mirrors and reflects the *consciousness* of Earth. Your feelings and emotions are the connection from your physical Self on Earth to your multi-dimensional DreamSelf that lies within. The reflective action of the Moon of solar light energy is how your DreamSelf knows exactly what is going on at any given moment within you and your life. The Moon acts as a *reflecting feedback system* sending your three dimensional Earth feelings and emotions back to your stellar DreamSelf that originates in the Milky Way Galaxy band of stars and beyond. This is also why gazing at the full moon always puts you in touch with your deepest feelings. You are sending them directly to your DreamSelf Within!

If we did not have the reflective action of the Moon cleansing, purifying, and deleting old programs from our three dimensional lives, we would be so bogged down that we wouldn't be able to move forward. So if you see a lot of cleansing and purification symbols in your dreams such as bathing, washing, or eliminating, you can bet and know it's a full moon! Two weeks after a full moon, the new moon will often show you dream themes of rebirth because a *new moon* heralds a new cycle of energy for you and your three-dimensional life. New moon dream themes usually have symbols of babies and children. The dream symbol of a baby or babies in your dream represents rebirth taking place within you and your life. Children as dream symbols represent your young and yet to be developed talents and abilities within. Very interesting!

In summary, looking again at *figure 2.9*, this over-all illustration shows that located within is your unlimited, multi-dimensional DreamSelf that is a complete system that eternally sustains Itself! This illustration also demonstrates how the energies of the Milky Way Galaxy of Stars, the Sun, and our Earth are mirror image multi-dimensional energies located and being reflected from within you!

Chakras—Your Non-Physical to Physical Energy Connections Within

Now that you are getting the *bigger picture* of what kind of energy you and your dreams are made of and how your dream energy creates your everyday physical Self and life, you may wonder how your extraordinary dream energy, as it slows down in vibration, actually connects to the "physical you" in the third dimension? And why, of course, would knowing this information be important as the next step in learning the Dreamtime Method, which accurately interprets your dreams?

Your non-physical, multi-dimensional dream energy connects to you in the physical third dimension through energy centers in your body called *chakras*. Knowing where your chakras are located in your body and their purpose is important because these energy centers, when shown to you in your dreams, provide you with specific information to assist you in interpreting your dreams accurately.

The definition of a *chakra* can be understood as being a portal that is a circular vortex of energy multi-dimensionally located within you. It is at these main vortexes of energy that your non-physical, multi-dimensional DreamSelf and dream energy, as it slows down in vibration becomes you, your physical Self and body here in the third dimension. To visualize this, look at *figure 2.10* on page 25.

In *figure 2.10*, as you start with the top of the figure's head in the illustration, I have your *Crown Chakra* labeled with the number "7." Multi-dimensionally, the energy of your Crown Chakra is the cosmic, nuclear energy of the Milky Way Galaxy band of stars and beyond. Your Crown Chakra is the location of your non-physical inner Dreamtime and is the galactic command center of your DreamSelf Within.

Your Crown Chakra energy is your *Creator Energy Within*, which mirrors the *Mind of the Creator*. It is the consciousness of your DreamSelf and your *Spiritual Sight Within*. Spiritual Sight is the *conscious* three-dimensional understanding that all energy that you now perceive as being outside of yourself and your physical body in the third-dimension is, in multi-dimensional reality, coming from the faster vibrating energy of your 10th dimensional Self, your DreamSelf Within. You open your Crown Chakra energy by interpreting your dreams using the Dreamtime Method and then connecting your dream information to your everyday physical Self and life.

➻ Three-dimensionally, you connect with your Crown Chakra's energy through interpreting your dreams consciously. You also connect with your Crown Chakra energy by your own physical vision of the Milky Way Galaxy band of stars and beyond. In *figure 2.10*, the stars of the Milky Way Galaxy are surrounding the top of the figure's head (#7).

➻ As you learn the Dreamtime Method (interpreting your dream symbols multi-dimensionally), and then connect your interpreted dream information to your three-dimensional Self and life, it activates and opens your Crown Chakra energy, your Creator Energy, your Spiritual Sight within. As your Crown Chakra energy activates and opens, you will feel it as a physical vibration coming from the top of your head.

➻ The color vibration associated with the Crown Chakra in the physical, third dimension is white.

Going from the top of the figure's head down, the next chakra illustrated in *figure 2.10* is your *Third-Eye Chakra*, labeled with the number "6." Multi-dimensionally, your Third-Eye Chakra is also the cosmic energy of the Milky Way Galaxy band of stars and beyond. Three-dimensionally, you connect with your Third Eye Chakra energy the same way you do with your Crown Chakra, by interpreting your dreams consciously. You also connect with your Third-Eye Chakra energy by your actual physical vision of the Milky Way Galaxy band of stars.

As you use the Dreamtime Method and learn to multi-dimensionally think as your DreamSelf Within does to interpret your dream symbols, you activate your Third-Eye Chakra energy within your three dimensional Self and life. As you open your Third-Eye Chakra energy center, it activates your Crown Chakra energy (which is the understanding of Spiritual Sight noted above).

↦ *Figure 2.10* illustrates your Third-Eye Chakra (#6) as surrounded by the stars of the Milky Way Galaxy and connected to your physical forehead.

↦ As you learn the Dreamtime Method to multi-dimensionally interpret your dreams and dream symbols, your Third-Eye Chakra energy opens activating your Crown Chakra energy. You will physically feel your Third-Eye Chakra energy as a strong energy vibration emanating from your forehead area.

↦ The color vibration associated with the Third-Eye Chakra in the physical, third dimension is purple.

Next in *figure 2.10* is your Throat Chakra, number "5." Multi-dimensionally, the energy of your Throat Chakra is the solar energy of the Sun. As noted earlier, the source of you and your DreamSelf's energy originates as nuclear star energy. As the energy of you and your DreamSelf's star consciousness (your dreams) moves on in vibration, it three-dimensionally becomes the solar energy of the Sun. The Sun, then, is the connecting portal where your dream energy passes from the non-physical energy of your DreamSelf Within to you and your physical body in the third dimension. Just as the Sun connects the Milky Way Galaxy band of stars to the Earth, your 5th chakra, the Throat Chakra, connects the upper (6 and 7th chakras) in your physical body to your lower chakras (4, 3, 2 and 1) in your physical body.

↦ Your Throat Chakra energy is your ability to speak, communicate, to "create and manifest" in the physical third dimension. This energy is the seat of your creativity within.

↦ Three dimensionally, you experience the energy of your throat chakra by your

24

Figure 2.10

"Chakras" – Your Energy Connection Centers From 10th Dimensional DreamSelf To Physical Self In The 3rd Dimension

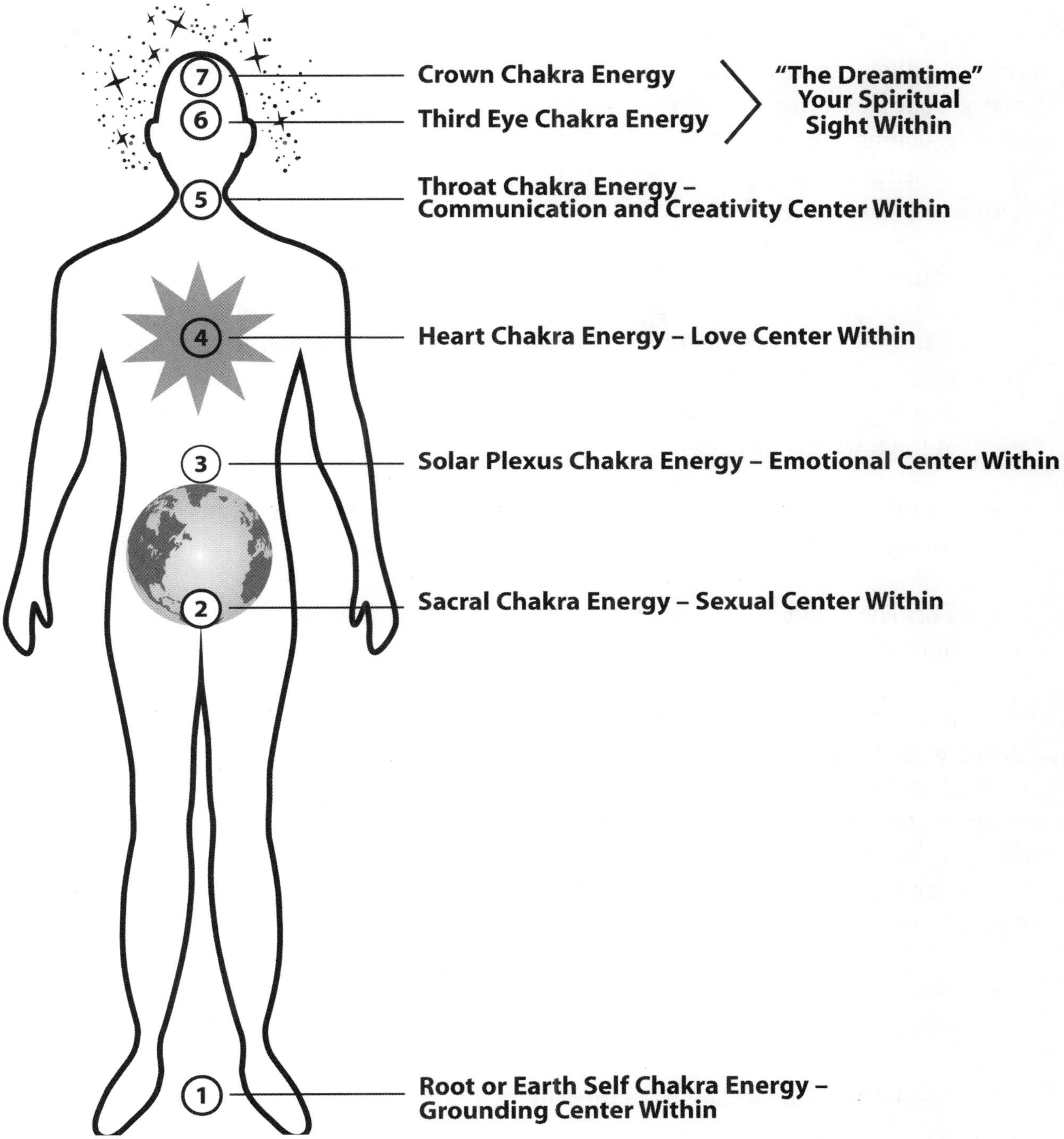

⑦ Crown Chakra Energy

⑥ Third Eye Chakra Energy

"The Dreamtime" Your Spiritual Sight Within

⑤ Throat Chakra Energy – Communication and Creativity Center Within

④ Heart Chakra Energy – Love Center Within

③ Solar Plexus Chakra Energy – Emotional Center Within

② Sacral Chakra Energy – Sexual Center Within

① Root or Earth Self Chakra Energy – Grounding Center Within direct physical vision and feel of the Sun (#5). As this chakra opens and operates in the third dimension, you physically feel it as an energy vibration emanating at the level of your throat.

⇒ The color vibration associated with the Throat Chakra in the physical, third dimension is blue.

In *figure 2.10*, the next chakra energy is your *Heart Chakra*, number "4." Multi-dimensionally, your Heart Chakra shares the energy of the Sun with your Throat Chakra energy. Your Heart Chakra energy connects to you in the physical third dimension by your actual vision and feel of the Sun. As your stellar DreamSelf and dream energy vibrates and becomes solar energy, it connects with you in the physical third dimension at the level of your heart (and throat, as indicated above).

⇒ Your Heart Chakra's energy is your three-dimensional ability to express Divine Love to yourself in your everyday physical life. The energy of this chakra is also your ability to love the *whole* of your multi-dimensional Self within, or the rest of yourself within. The "rest of yourself within" being understood as all of the energy you now perceive as *being separate* from you and your physical Self and life in the third dimension.

⇒ As this chakra opens and operates in the third dimension, it is physically felt as an energy vibration coming from the level of your heart (#4).

⇒ The color vibration associated with the Heart Chakra in the physical, third dimension is green.

In *figure 2.10*, your next chakra's energy is your *Solar Plexus Chakra*, which I have labeled with the number "3." Multi-dimensionally, your Solar Plexus Chakra energy is the physical energy of the Earth. Your Solar Plexus Chakra's energy is three-dimensionally connected to you in your body at your physical stomach area. As your dream energy is absorbed into the spiraling light encoded filaments of the DNA of your physical body at your Solar plexus area (your gut or stomach area), it connects to you by your actual physical vision and contact with the energy of Earth.

⇒ Your Solar Plexus Chakra's energy is your Emotional Self and your intuition. This chakra's energy, your gut feeling, is very accurate for prediction and knowing.

⇒ As this chakra opens and operates in the third dimension, it is physically felt as an energy vibration at the level of your gut area (#3).

→ The color vibration associated with the Solar Plexus Chakra in the physical, third dimension is yellow.

In *figure 2.10*, your next chakra's energy is your *Sacral Chakra*, labeled as number "2." Multi-dimensionally, your Sacral Chakra energy is also the physical energy of Earth. Your Sacral Chakra's energy is three-dimensionally connected to you in your physical body at your pelvic or groin area. As your dream energy is absorbed into the spiraling light encoded filaments of the DNA of your physical body at your sacral area (groin), it connects to you by your actual physical vision and contact with the energy of Earth.

→ Your Sacral Chakra's energy is your Sexual Self-energy, your physical ability to create, procreate, and to make your creativity manifest/happen in the third dimension.

→ The energy of the Sacral Chakra is to ground your creativity in the physical. As this chakra opens and operates in the third dimension, it is physically felt as an energy vibration in your groin area (#2).

→ The color vibration associated with the Sacral Chakra in the physical, third dimension is orange.

Lastly, in *figure 2.10*, your "base" chakra energy, called your *Root or Earth Self Chakra* is labeled number "1." Multi-dimensionally, your Root Chakra energy is again the physical energy of Earth. Your Root Chakra's energy is three-dimensionally connected to you in your body at the base of your physical spine. As your dream energy is absorbed into the spiraling light encoded filaments of the DNA of your physical body at the base of your spine, it connects to you by your actual physical vision and contact with the energy of Earth.

→ Your Root Chakra's energy is your ability to stay grounded and in the physical. It is your deepest energy connection to the crystalline core of Mother Earth.

→ As this chakra opens and operates in the third dimension, it is physically felt as an energy vibration in your spine and at your feet (#1).

→ The color vibration associated with the Root Chakra in the physical, third dimension is red.

As you learn to understand what your dreams mean, knowing what your chakras energy centers are, and where in your body they are located, will assist you in interpreting your dreams more clearly. For example, if you dreamed of an arrow being shot into your throat, your DreamSelf would be telling you that there is a pointed and sharp issue regarding your ability to communicate that is now going on within you and your three-dimensional life. The dream symbol of your throat would be symbolizing the energy of your *throat chakra* and your ability to create and communicate.

I would like you now to take an over-all look back at *figure 2.10* on page 25. This important illustration shows how your DreamSelf's 10th dimensional, faster vibrating non-physical dream energy connects three dimensionally with the slower vibrating energy that is you and your physical body. This illustration also shows you how you can think and imagine the cosmic energy of the Milky Way Galaxy, our Sun, and Earth as all being multi-dimensional mirror image energies that are three-dimensionally being reflected out *from within you!*

Your Supernatural Multi-Dimensional DreamSelf Within

In closing Chapter Two, I would like you to go outside tonight and look up at the stars of the Milky Way Galaxy and beyond. You can look up at these beautiful stars and think of them differently now. You can know that these extraordinary star energies are the birthplace of you and your Divine, multi-dimensional DreamSelf Within, the Creator of you and your three-dimensional life.

Tomorrow when you go outside and feel the sun's rays on your face or see the shimmering sunlight that grows your garden, you can know that our magnificent Sun is an energy center of Light (and information) that multi-dimensionally lies within you.

And . . . as you stand on Mother Earth every day, you can know that grounding your multi-dimensional energy on this beautiful planet is what you are meant to be doing right now. That the beauty of the Earth reflects the evolving foundation of your super-natural, multi-dimensional DreamSelf Within.

I'm so glad that you have taken the time to read this important chapter in order to recognize yourself as a Multi-Dimensional Energy Being. This truthful understanding is the foundation and key to interpreting your dreams easily, accurately, and multi-dimensionally.

But wait . . . what is that loud noise that we hear? It sounds like a huge alarm clock ticking off!

Right now, a very loud alarm clock is ticking off within the multi-dimensions of you. Could that huge alarm clock going off have anything to do with why in your life right now you seek the knowledge of how to interpret your dreams?

I'll see you in Chapter Three!

Learning the Dreamtime Method and Tapping into Your Dreamtime Consciousness Within

"Going home."

Once upon a time, the Creator created a galaxy: a *free-will place* where all that is desired could be created! This creative place was left to grow and be all that it could be. Every now and then, a new and higher order of evolution came to be in this creative place.

Ultimately, it was planned, that a time in the ages would come when this creative galaxy would continue to be a free-will place, but also become *complete by joining together with itself.* As this occasion neared, there was considerable preparation going on. There was much tidying up and putting things in order, so to say. It was also a time of great anticipation and joy, since for eons everyone, all energy in the galaxy, had anticipated this aligning convergence within.

But what was this "big event," *this completed joining together* to mean for the galaxy? It was to mean that this would be the time when all of the galaxy would come to *consciously understand* that it is the original Creator of all that has been created! This was the time for the galaxy to deeply understand that there is *no other* doing the creating, that you are the Creator of all that has been created. That all creations *return home* to the Creator . . . and that Self is now meeting Self!

This was a time for a most profound comprehension for the galaxy. A time marked by deep healing in the understanding, the *remembrance* and the *recognition* of one's true Divine, Multi-Dimensional Self that lies within. A time of fulfillment to that understanding, which also meant a *new beginning!* It was a great time to be alive and well in the galaxy, as that time . . . *is now!*

As you learn to use the Dreamtime Method to accurately interpret your dreams, you will find yourself experiencing an extraordinary mind-expanding awareness! The reason this occurs as you master the Dreamtime Method and learn to *think* as your DreamSelf Within is that you bring the faster vibrating 10th dimensional light energy of your DreamSelf *consciously* to your everyday physical, three-dimensional Self. The consciousness of your DreamSelf brings to your awareness the power of how you are the Creator of your three-dimensional Self and life!

When I first started interpreting my own dreams using my Dreamtime Method, I was in complete awe that my dreams related *exactly to what was going on within my life*. I also quickly came to understand and realize that there were just no coincidences going on within myself or life.

An example of this that I can give to you is if I was *thinking* I needed to contact a plumber to fix my plumbing, low and behold in the next few days, I either received a call from a plumber soliciting business or received something from a plumber or plumbing business in the mail! I thought, wow, I was just *thinking of that!* Another example was that again, maybe I was "thinking" of calling a friend or family member and out of the blue, they called me. I had a lot of these kinds of experiences that we all have every day, but what had changed as I interpreted my dreams was that I was definitely more aware that this type of synchronicity was happening within my life. Was this just coincidence or was I becoming more telepathic and clairvoyant? What I found, as I interpreted my dreams and connected the interpreted dream information to my everyday life, was that I was definitely becoming more conscious of how energy flowed around and within my life.

Your Extraordinary Multi-Dimensional Alignment Occurring Within

In Chapter Two, I demonstrated to you *that you are a Multi-Dimensional Energy Being*. I did this by having you think and imagine the star energy of the Milky Way Galaxy as being a multi-dimensional *mirror image* of your three-dimensional Self. That although from the physical world the star energies of the Milky Way Galaxy appear to be outside of you, they are in truth a multi-dimensional reflection of your physical, three-dimensional Self's Crown and Third-Eye chakra energies.

I then had you envision the Milky Way Galaxy of stars spiraling out on its vibrational pathway connecting to the solar energy of the Sun—with the solar energy of our Sun being a multi-dimensional mirror image of your physical, three-dimensional Self's Throat and Heart Chakra energies.

Lastly, I went on to have you imagine the solar energy of the Sun flowing down as light energy to Earth—with the energy of Earth being a multi-dimensional reflection of your physical, three-dimensional Self's Solar Plexus, Sacral and Root chakra energies.

Right now as humanity enters the next stage of evolution, our *Age of Light*, your physical three-dimensional Self and consciousness is coming to an *evolutionary return*. This extraordinary return is being symbolized by a rare and on-going astronomical *alignment* of the Earth and the solstice Sun to the Galactic Center of the Milky Way Galaxy of stars, illustrated for you on the cover of this book and again in *figure 3.1*.

Now, as you look at *figure 3.1* and envision the energy of the Milky Way Galaxy of stars, the solar energy of the Sun, and the planetary energy of the Earth all positioning

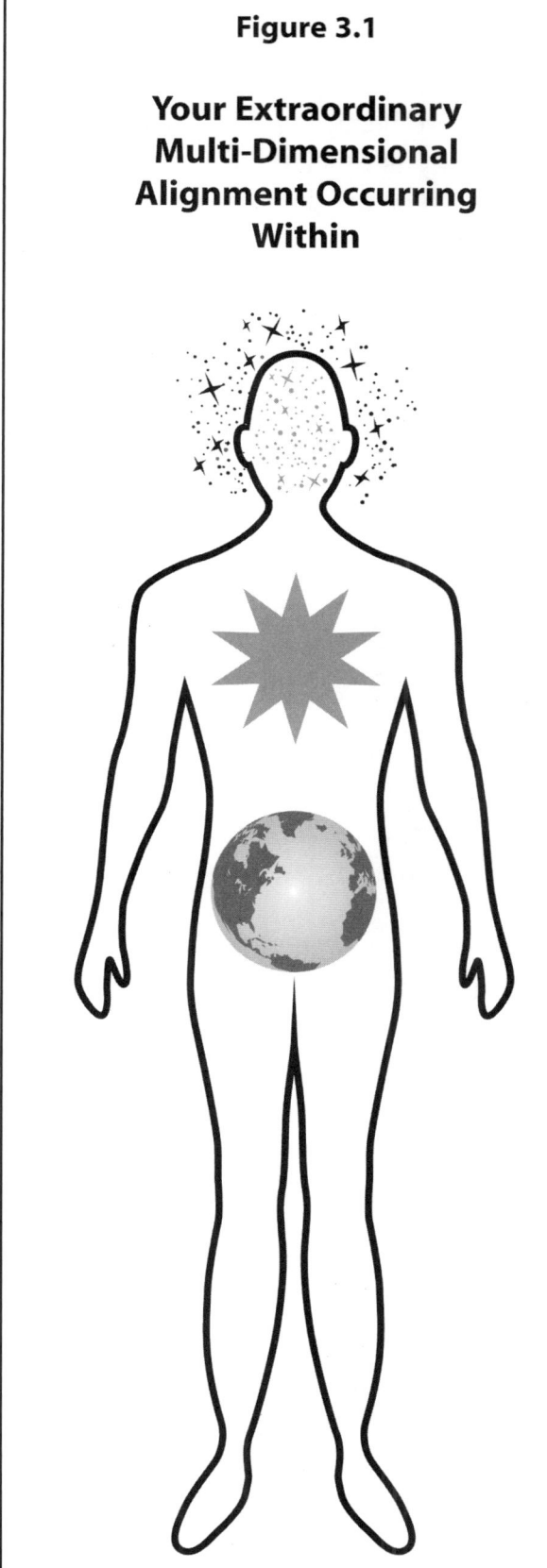

Figure 3.1

Your Extraordinary Multi-Dimensional Alignment Occurring Within

into a rare alignment, while at the same time understanding that these aligning energies are mirroring your *own multi-dimensional energies within*, what might this extraordinary alignment symbolize in terms of what is now occurring within you?

The current aligning of the galactic center of the Milky Way Galaxy with the Sun and Earth says that your multi-dimensional DreamSelf (symbolized by Milky Way Galaxy star energy) and your everyday physical Self and life (symbolized by Sun and Earth energy) are now being impulsed into *perfect synchronization together*. This means that your current, everyday consciousness is being raised to that of your DreamSelf Within to reveal that you are not merely a physical being who lives only in the third dimension. The remarkable astronomical alignment visualized and noted above is communicating that you have a non-physical, multi-dimensional counterpart, your DreamSelf Within, whose supernatural consciousness is physically joining together with your present, everyday three dimensional consciousness now.

The on-going planetary alignment of the Earth and the solstice Sun with the Galactic Center of the Milky Way Galaxy of stars is the huge alarm clock that is *ticking away* within you now! As your multi-dimensional energies symbolically reflected to you in the third dimension by the Earth, the Sun and the galactic center of the Milky Way Galaxy come into harmonic alignment, your inner DreamSelf and the Dreamtime also come into harmonic alignment becoming the new reality of your present everyday three-dimensional Self's consciousness. You wanting to learn what your dreams mean and how to interpret them is by no mistake or accident! As humanity enters the Age of Light, *your Age of Alignment Within*, and you reunite with your multi-dimensional DreamSelf now being activated and symbolized by the on-going planetary alignment, you are being *regenerated* by a direct flow of extraordinary energy. This extraordinary energy is quickening your interest in consciously learning the language of your DreamSelf, which are your dreams.

Your DreamSelf's Thinking and Consciousness, Your "Spiritual Sight" Within

The Dreamtime Method of interpreting your dreams is learning to think and understand your dreams just as your multi-dimensional DreamSelf Within does so that you can interpret them accurately. As you interpret your dreams using the Dreamtime Method and consciously connect the information and guidance of them to your everyday Self and life, you absorb the faster vibrating light energy of your DreamSelf Within, raising your physical vibration in the third dimension to that of your 10th dimensional Self. As this happens, the heightened vibration of your DreamSelf Within opens your Third-Eye Chakra energy which in turn activates your Crown Chakra energy. Your Crown Chakra energy is your *Creator energy within, your Spiritual Sight*, the super-consciousness of you and your DreamSelf Within.

Turn now to *figure 3.2* on page 33. *Figure 3.2* is your Multi-Dimensional DreamSelf's "View and Perspective" that we looked at in Chapter Two. I am showing you this visual again because I want you to now look at *figure 3.2* as being an *illustrated definition* of your DreamSelf's 10th dimensional Crown and Third-Eye chakra energies, your Spiritual Sight within.

Spiritual Sight is your conscious three-dimensional understanding that all energy that you now perceive as being outside of yourself and your physical body in the third-dimension is, in multi-dimensional reality, being created and coming from the faster vibrating, non-physical energy of your 10th dimensional Self, your DreamSelf Within. This understanding says that as your DreamSelf's 10th dimensional energy slows in vibration becoming the third-dimension, your DreamSelf accordingly perceives all energies of the third dimension as being actual physical aspects and abilities of you and itself. Your DreamSelf thinks in this way because multi-dimensionally, these energies are! In *figure 3.2*, you can visualize this by seeing how your 10th dimensional DreamSelf, as it looks into its and your "three-dimensional mirror," views all energies of the physical world as being *aspects of its (and your) 10th multi-dimensional power from within*.

The above understanding of Spiritual Sight translates to mean that as your DreamSelf creates your dreams for you, it thinks of your dream symbols as though each is then an actual aspect of the *physical power, energy, and ability* of you and itself. And for you to interpret your dream symbols multi-dimensionally and accurately, you must think and perceive your dream symbols in the very same way!

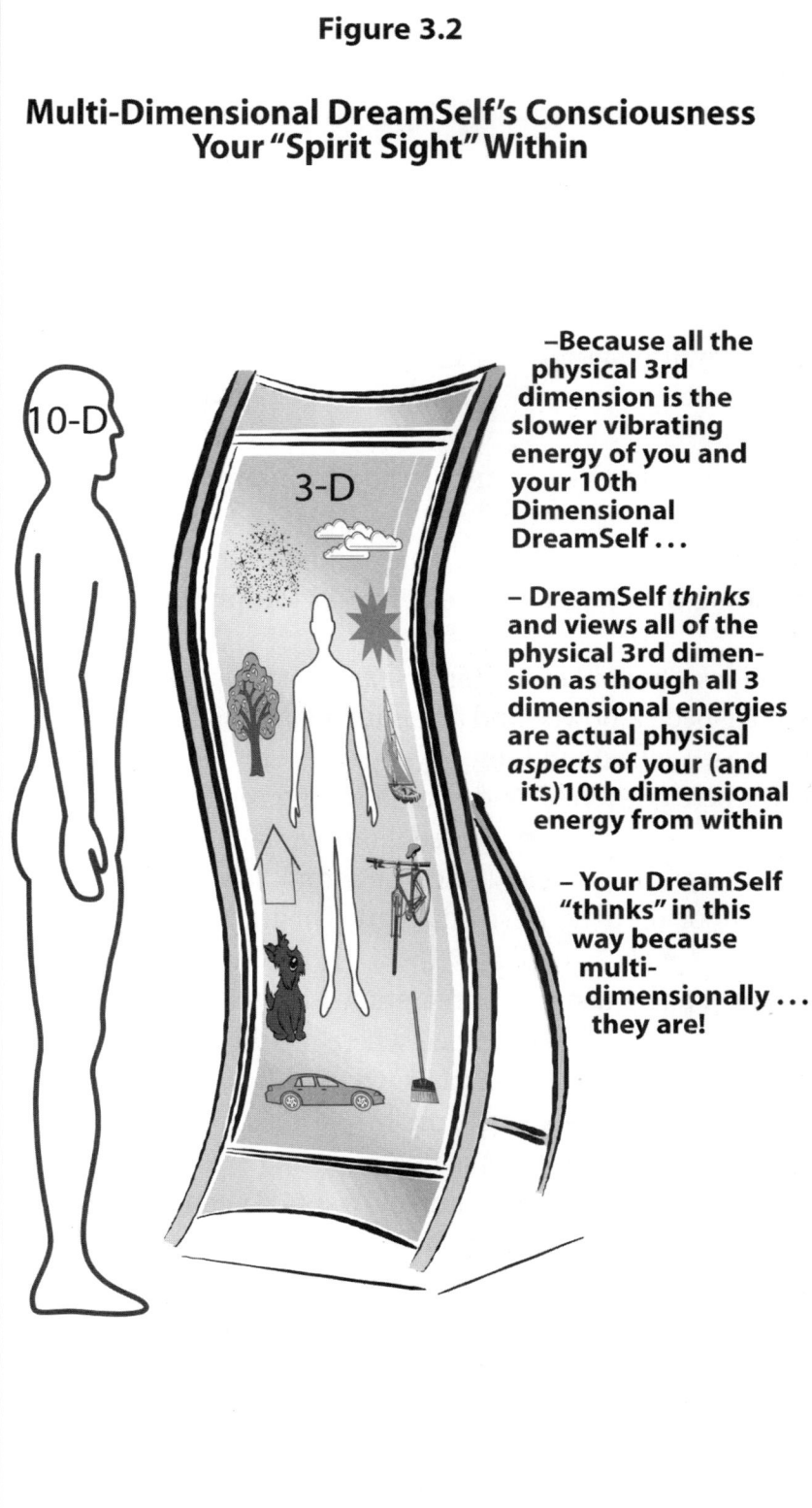

Figure 3.2

Multi-Dimensional DreamSelf's Consciousness Your "Spirit Sight" Within

10-D

3-D

–Because all the physical 3rd dimension is the slower vibrating energy of you and your 10th Dimensional DreamSelf . . .

– DreamSelf *thinks* and views all of the physical 3rd dimension as though all 3 dimensional energies are actual physical *aspects* of your (and its)10th dimensional energy from within

– Your DreamSelf "thinks" in this way because multi-dimensionally . . . they are!

Thinking as Your DreamSelf Does—The Dreamtime Method of Interpreting Your Dreams

As you learn the Dreamtime Method and begin to "think" as your DreamSelf Within does, the method and *way of thinking* you will use is to imagine that *you are the central creator* of your dreamed dream. Each of your dream symbols is then a *physical creation, a part of you* that you have produced! This means that each dream symbol in your dream should be interpreted as being a physical aspect, a physical power, and a physical ability that you now have and possess from within.

Taking the above understandings together, for you to receive an accurate interpretation of your dream symbols and "think" as your DreamSelf Within does, you will start by taking the normal, three-dimensional definition of your dream symbol. You then look at that particular definition/meaning as though it is an actual aspect of physical power and ability that you now possess from within.

Keeping the above *way of thinking* in mind, the Dreamtime Method for accurately interpreting your dreams and *thinking* as your DreamSelf Within does proceeds as follows:

→ You start by taking the normal three-dimensional definition and understanding for your dream symbol.

→ You then think of that understanding as though you *are* the actual physical, three-dimensional energy of your dream symbol. By "thinking" in this way, you interpret your dream symbol as your DreamSelf created it.

→ As you *think in this way*, the information attained gives you an absolutely accurate interpretation of your dream symbol!

The following is an example using the Dreamtime Method to interpret a dream symbol.

I will start with the common dream symbol of a *house*. The everyday, three-dimensional definition and understanding of a house can be defined as "a physical place where one lives."

I then think of this meaning as my DreamSelf Within *thinks* of it. That the dream symbol of the house is now a physical aspect, a power, and an ability of my own everyday three-dimensional energy that I now possess from within.

If a house is a "physical place where one lives," and I am now a house, the physical place where I *live* in the third-dimension is within me, my three-dimensional body, and my everyday life. This means that the interpretation that I then get from thinking as my DreamSelf does about the dream symbol of a house is that my DreamSelf wants to communicate information to me . . . *about me!*

How I came to this understanding was by using the Dreamtime Method and thinking as my DreamSelf Within does. If a house is "a physical place where one lives" and I am now the actual *physical* energy of the house, the physical place where I live in the third-dimension is within the energy of me, my physical body, and my three-dimensional life. So, by *thinking in this way*, the only logical conclusion I can come up with using the Dreamtime Method for the dream symbol of a house is that my DreamSelf wants to communicate information to me about *me, my physical body and my everyday three-dimensional life*.

I now want you to look at *figure 3.3* on page 35. In *figure 3.3*, I have illustrated along the *outside outline* of the form the faster vibrating, non-physical energy of my 10th dimensional DreamSelf Within. As my DreamSelf's 10th dimensional energy slows down in vibration and becomes the third dimension as viewed within the outline of the form, my DreamSelf perceives me (and it) as the solid, physical energy of the third dimension.

From my DreamSelf's 10th dimensional perspective, "the place" where it lives, its

Figure 3.3

How Your DreamSelf Perceives The Physical 3rd Dimension And "Creates" Your Dream Symbols

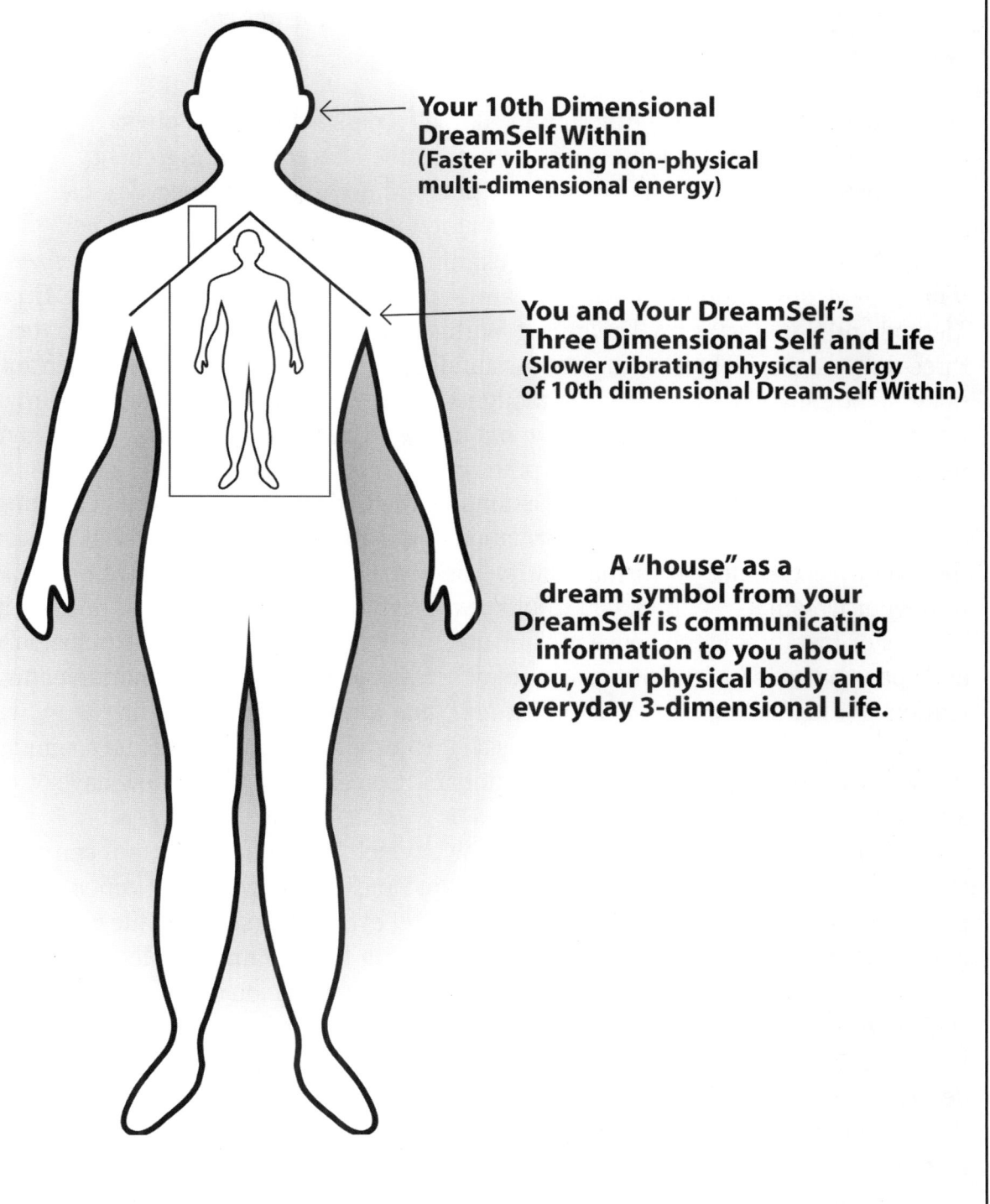

Your 10th Dimensional DreamSelf Within
(Faster vibrating non-physical multi-dimensional energy)

You and Your DreamSelf's Three Dimensional Self and Life
(Slower vibrating physical energy of 10th dimensional DreamSelf Within)

A "house" as a dream symbol from your DreamSelf is communicating information to you about you, your physical body and everyday 3-dimensional Life.

"house" so to speak, is within the slower vibrating energy of its three-dimensional Self, which is me, my physical body, and my life.

→ Thus, as illustrated in *figure 3.3*, from my DreamSelf's perspective and view of the third-dimension, the communication of the dream symbol of a house to mean me, my physical body, and my three-dimensional life is *absolutely correct and accurate in its interpretation!*

→ This is *true* because from my DreamSelf's perspective, the "physical place" where it lives in the third-dimension is within the slower vibrating energy of its three-dimensional Self, which is me, my physical body, and my everyday life.

As you can see from the above example, I received a *correct and accurate multi-dimensional interpretation* of my dream symbol of a house by using the Dreamtime Method and thinking as my DreamSelf Within does. I did this easily by taking the normal three-dimensional definition and understanding for my dream symbol. I then took that understanding and thought of it as though I was the actual physical energy of my dream symbol. In imagining that *I was now the actual physical energy* of my dream symbol, I received an absolutely accurate interpretation of it!

Now, once you have used the Dreamtime Method and understood that a "house" as a dream symbol is communicating information to you about "you, your physical Self, and your three-dimensional life," to further clarify your dream symbol communication of a house, from your DreamSelf Within, you would next need to look at *what kind* of a house it is.

For instance, is the house in your dream a large house, possibly a mansion? A rich and spacious house would interpret to mean that your DreamSelf is communicating information to you about your *wealthy, abundant, and unlimited* Self within.

Or is your house a small shack, which then would be symbolizing and communicating to you the current *poor and limited* thinking and perception that you now have of yourself and your everyday life.

Does your house have lots of windows which would interpret to mean your inner ability to see *outside* of yourself at this present time. Or, no windows, which would interpret to mean you being "closed" off from seeing beyond yourself and life at this time.

As you interpret your dream symbols using the Dreamtime Method, be aware of the *details* surrounding them. Whether your house is a mansion or a shack gives you *more information* of what your DreamSelf is specifically saying to you that is mirroring what is presently going on within you and your everyday three-dimensional life. Whatever the descriptions surrounding your dream symbols, make sure you include these details and their appropriate interpreted meanings to get an accurate understanding of the information being communicated by your DreamSelf in your dream.

Remember earlier in Chapter Two when I said that your dreams and dream symbols not only *tell* you what is going on within your Self and your life, but as your own 10th dimensional power of light energy go on to create in the third dimension? In the above example of dreaming of a mansion-type house, you as the dreamer in your next day and days after dreaming your dream should look for the energies of expansion, abundance, and wealth (similar and "like" energy) to be present in and around you and your everyday life. These specific energies were created and attracted to you in the third dimension by your 10th dimensional DreamSelf's dream symbol communication of your "mansion-type house" (a mansion translating to and equaling: abundance and wealth).

As the 10th dimensional light energy of your dream symbols slow down in vibration to become you and your three dimensional life, they, as energy, go on to attract to you in the third dimension the energies of whatever you are dreaming of and in the case of the mansion-type house, the energies of expansion, abundance, and wealth. It is in this way that your dream symbols as living energy, *create* you and your life in the third dimension.

The extra added benefit of interpreting your dream symbols and *consciously knowing* what they mean as in the above example of a "mansion-type house" is that they mindfully will assist you *to be aware* when the opportunities of abundance and expansion present themselves in your life for you to then *consciously* take advantage of them. And in stating this you'll become more conscious of changes that you need to make in your life to attain them. This would be in contrast to the common everyday three-dimensional thinking or understanding that life is just a matter of *luck or coincidence*, which it isn't! The valuable *awareness* that interpreting your dreams consciously brings to you is the *knowing confirmation* that you and your life are not just a matter of chaos or happenstance, but that *you are indeed the conscious "creator" of your three-dimensional Self and life*. That you are creating your Self and life by the very dreams you are dreaming and subsequent three-dimensional thoughts you are thinking!

Dreamtime Dream Symbol Template

For your learning and convenience, I have created a Dreamtime dream symbol "template" for interpreting each of your dream symbols using the Dreamtime Method. This template is an easy-to-use "pattern" where, as you are learning the Dreamtime Method, you can write in your dream symbols to be interpreted. The template allows you to fill in the form much as I did above when interpreting the dream symbol of a "house" using the Dreamtime Method.

The template form looks like the sample one on page 38.

Dreamtime Method Template

- **Using the Dreamtime Method, the normal, three-dimensional definition of**

  a _____ *(your dream symbol)* _____ **could be understood as a**

  _____ *(your dream symbol's three-dimensional definition)* _____ **.**

- **I then think of this definition/meaning as my DreamSelf within *thinks of***

  ***it*, which is as though the dream symbol of a** _____ *(your dream symbol)* _____

  is now a "physical aspect and ability" of my own three-dimensional

  energy that comes from within.

- **As I think of myself *being* the energy of the three-dimensional** _____

  _____ *(your dream symbol)* _____ **, the interpretation**

  that I get from "*thinking*" as my DreamSelf Within does is that for the

  dream symbol of a _____ *(your dream symbol)* _____ **,**

  my DreamSelf wants to communicate information to me about

  _____ *(your dream symbol's Dreamtime Dream Interpretation)* _____

  _____

  _____

  within my everyday Self and life.

As I move forward in this chapter, we will figure out more dream symbol examples using the Dreamtime Method. Starting on page 135 at the back of this book, I have included blank Dreamtime Method Template pages so that you can now go along and fill one out for each dream symbol we interpret in this chapter to get used to using the Dreamtime Method. Additional blank Dreamtime Method Template pages are also included there for you to use at a later time when interpreting your own dream symbols using the Dreamtime Method.

Your Dreamtime Dream Dictionary

Remember in Chapter One when I said you *will become* your own dream dictionary? Now that you have used the Dreamtime Method to interpret the first dream symbol of a "house" turn to *figure 3.4* below. This is a sample of a page that I have labeled: "My Dreamtime Dream Dictionary."

As I have figured out my first dream symbol using the Dreamtime Method, I want to remember what I interpreted that symbol to mean. So, on the left side of the page, I write the word "house." I put the equal (=) sign next to the word. I then write the meaning of the dream symbol of the house as interpreted by using the Dreamtime Method. My Dreamtime Dream Dictionary page looks just like *figure 3.4* below.

As we continue on now learning the Dreamtime Method to individually interpret each of your dream symbols (how to interpret dream sentences and paragraphs using the Dreamtime Method will follow in Chapter Four), *I strongly suggest* that you create pages to be used as your own "Dreamtime Dream Dictionary."

This is a good idea because writing down the meaning of the specific dream symbol will assist you in recalling the interpretation when you experience that dream symbol again in another dream. When you have a dream symbol communicated that you have already interpreted from an earlier dream, you can reference back to your dream dictionary to refresh yourself on its meaning. Also, the very act of writing down your dream symbols and their meanings grounds the energy of your dream symbol within you, mentally, physically, and spiritually (non-physically).

Included in this book starting on page 125 are pages labeled "My Dreamtime Dream Dictionary." As you learn to interpret your dream symbols using the Dreamtime Method, this section is there for you to write down your Dreamtime dream symbols and interpretations that you have "figured out," so take a look at these pages!

Figure 3.4

My Dreamtime Dream Dictionary

House =   **A communication from my DreamSelf regarding me, my physical body, and my everyday life (you, your physical body and your everyday life).**

The Automatic Nature of Your Dream Symbols

Something that you will notice as you become familiar with the Dreamtime Method and interpret your dream symbols is that once you have interpreted a dream symbol and its meaning, that *understanding and definition* will always be the meaning you will use to interpret and relate to your specific dream symbol. A "house" as a dream symbol meaning *you, your physical body, and life* will always be the interpretation you should use in any future dreams when the dream symbol of a house presents itself. So the good news in interpreting your dream symbols is that once you have interpreted a dream symbol's meaning, it will always refer to and have that specific generic meaning and understanding in any of your future dreams! Your descriptions surrounding your dream symbol (as in our dream symbol example of the house) may vary, but a "house" as a dream symbol will always be communicating information to you about you and your everyday, physical life.

The "other" good news regarding your dream symbols is that the more that you interpret them in your dreams, the interpretation you arrive at for any specific dream symbol will then become *automatic* within you. The reason this happens as you interpret your dreams is because you are erasing the *invisible layers* between your 10th dimensional DreamSelf and your everyday Self in the third dimension. Remember, as you interpret your dreams, you raise your physical vibration in the third-dimension to that of your 10th dimensional Self *becoming* your DreamSelf's consciousness within your everyday Self and life. By using the Dreamtime Method and learning to interpret your dreams, you become *unlimited and all-knowing* just as your DreamSelf Within.

Interpreting Your Dream Symbols Using the Dreamtime Method

Now that we have interpreted our first dream symbol of a "house," to mean me, my physical body, and my three-dimensional life (you, your physical body, and your three-dimensional life), as we continue learning the Dreamtime Method to interpret each of your dream symbols, how might we interpret the *rooms* in the house?

Since a "house" as a dream symbol from my DreamSelf's perspective and thinking represents me or myself, could the different rooms in the house in my dream be symbolizing different parts of myself and my everyday life?

To find out, let's imagine that in my dream I now am in the living room of the house. I will use the Dreamtime Method to interpret what the dream symbol of a "living room" of a house means.

(Reader, use a blank Dreamtime Method Template page as noted above located starting on page 135 to fill out as we now go along and interpret the dream symbol of a living room of a house).

Thinking as my DreamSelf Within does, I take the normal physical, three-dimensional definition and understanding of a "living room" of a house. The definition of a living room is usually thought of as the "center" of a house. I then think of its meaning as my DreamSelf Within *thinks*, which is as though the dream symbol of the "living room" is now a "physical aspect, power, and ability" of my own three-dimensional energy within.

As I think of myself as *being* the energy of a three-dimensional living room and imagine myself now as the "center" of a house, the interpretation that I get from "thinking" as my DreamSelf Within does is that with the dream symbol of a "living room," my DreamSelf wants to communicate information to me that is now at the *"center"* of my (and its) three-dimensional Self and life.

How I intuit that this interpretation is correct and how I came to this understanding is because I already know from using the Dreamtime Method that a house from my DreamSelf *symbolizes* me. So, if a house symbolizes me and my life, and the living room of a three-dimensional house is its *center*, then the interpretation of a "living room" from my DreamSelf is communicating information to me that is at the "center" of me and my three-dimensional life.

Now turn to *figure 3.5* on page 43. As you can see illustrated in *figure 3.5*, a living room being perceived by my DreamSelf as "the center" of my (and its) three-dimensional life is *absolutely accurate* in its interpretation.

⇢ This interpretation is correct because from my DreamSelf's 10th dimensional perspective, "the place" where it lives, its "house" so to speak, is within the slower vibrating energy of its three-dimensional Self, which is me, my physical body, and my life.

⇢ This understanding correspondingly means that the "center" of my DreamSelf's "house," its "living room" so to speak, is then within the "center" of my three-dimensional Self and life.

With the dream symbol of a "living room" of a house, my DreamSelf Within is communicating information that is *central and at the center* of what is now happening in my everyday three-dimensional life. To give you an example of why my DreamSelf may have communicated the dream symbol of a "living room" of a house by my actual dream of being in a living room could be that possibly I have been distracted by extraneous issues going on outside of myself and life. In this dream, my "living room" dream symbol is symbolizing and communicating this "central" issue to me, the fact that I am focusing elsewhere in my everyday living versus within the "center" of myself and life.

Now turn to the page you have titled "My Dreamtime Dream Dictionary" (or in this book starting on page 125 titled "My Dreamtime Dream Dictionary"). Write down the second dream symbol you have just interpreted using the Dreamtime Method, the symbol of a "living room." Next to this put the = sign and write the Dreamtime interpretation we just came up with for the dream symbol of a "living room." Your Dreamtime Dream Dictionary page should look like *figure 3.6* below.

Figure 3.6

My Dreamtime Dream Dictionary

House =   **A communication from my DreamSelf regarding me, my physical body, and my everyday life.**

Living Room =   **A communication from my DreamSelf regarding information that is going on within the "center" of myself and my life.**

The reason your DreamSelf uses every day, three-dimensional objects and events as dream symbols to communicate to you is because it knows that you, its *three-dimensional Self*, are most familiar in waking reality with the physical world. Your DreamSelf Within knows that by giving you everyday three-dimensional objects and events as dream symbols, *you will intuitively know* what the "three-dimensional definition and understanding" means and will realize what it is trying to say to you!

Now in the example of the dream symbol of the living room, was the "living room" in your house clean, large, and spacious? These descriptions of the living room can be interpreted to mean that within you right now, you feel clear (clean) about your life, you feel unlimited (large) and very open (spacious) regarding the central issues going within you and your three-dimensional life (the house). Or was the living room in your dream darkly lit? This would symbolize that at the center of your life right now (the living room), you have low awareness and energy (i.e., the living room being darkly lit with low light). This gives you an idea of how the basic interpretation of a dream symbol will remain constant and how you should then add the descriptions attached to your dream symbol to get a deeper understanding of information being communicated to you by your DreamSelf.

The Easy-to-Do Dreamtime Method of Interpreting Your Dream Symbols

Now, didn't I tell you that figuring out your dream symbols would be easy, fun, and accurate using the Dreamtime Method! To continue on, let's imagine that I am now leaving the living room of the house in my dream and am now in the bathroom of the house.

(Reader, use a blank Dreamtime Method Template page located starting on page 135 to fill out as we interpret the following dream symbol of a "bathroom" using the Dreamtime Method).

Figure 3.5

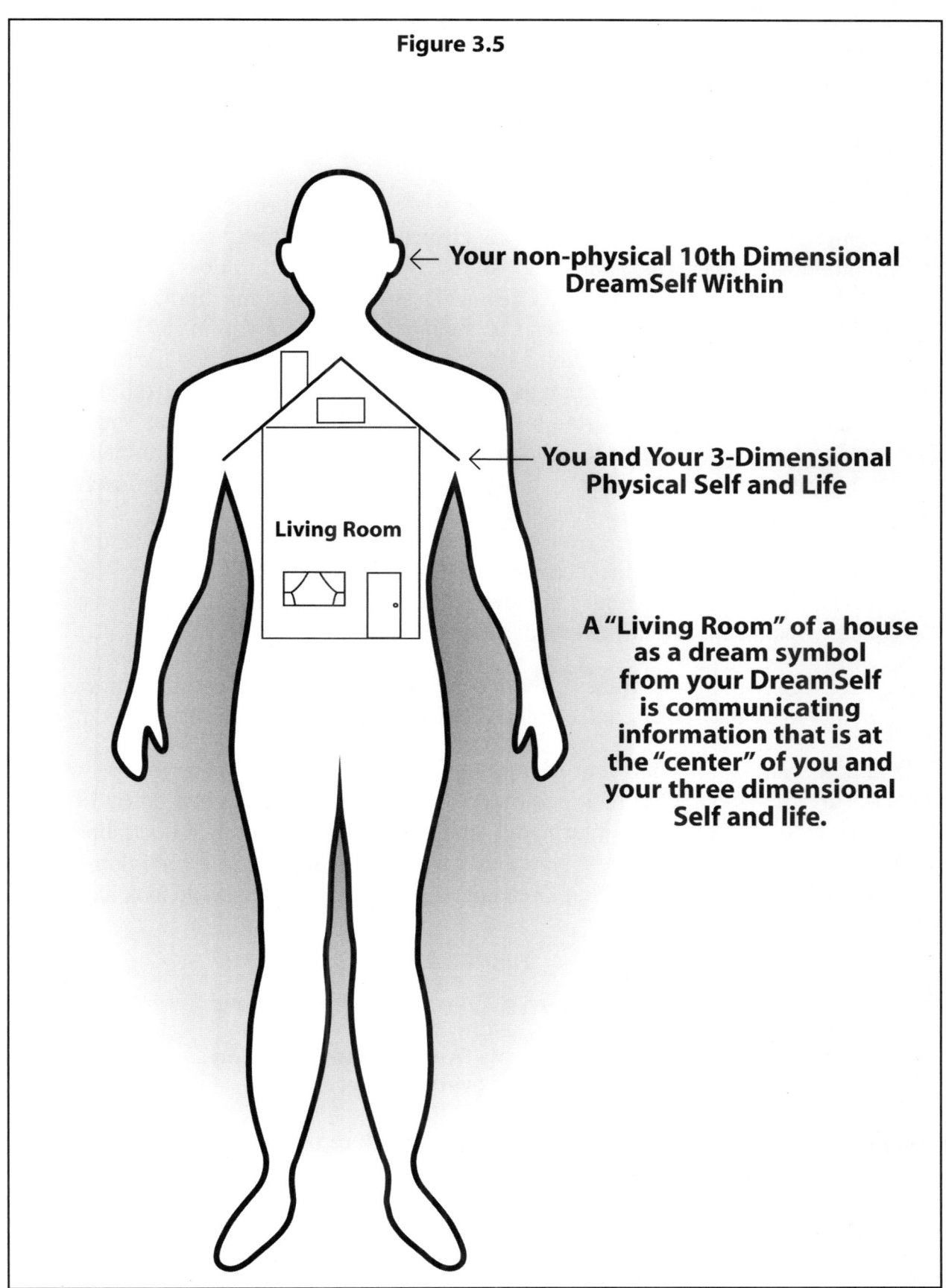

← Your non-physical 10th Dimensional DreamSelf Within

← You and Your 3-Dimensional Physical Self and Life

Living Room

A "Living Room" of a house as a dream symbol from your DreamSelf is communicating information that is at the "center" of you and your three dimensional Self and life.

Using the Dreamtime Method, the normal three-dimensional definition of a bathroom is "a place within a house used for cleansing, purification, and elimination."

I then think of this meaning as my DreamSelf Within *thinks* of it, which defines the dream symbol of the "bathroom" as a "physical aspect, power, and ability" of my own three-dimensional energy that comes from within.

As I think of myself as *being* the energy of a three-dimensional "bathroom" and imagine myself as "a place within a house for cleansing, purification, and elimination," the interpretation that I get from "thinking" as my DreamSelf Within does, for the dream symbol of a "bathroom," is that my DreamSelf is communicating information to me regarding my three-dimensional power and ability to be a place within my own Self of cleansing, purification, and elimination for my everyday physical Self and life (the house).

Again, intuit this interpretation as *correct* because I already know from using the Dreamtime Method that a house from my DreamSelf symbolizes me. And, as you can see illustrated in *figure 3.7* on page 45, a bathroom being perceived by my DreamSelf as my three-dimensional power and ability to be a place within me of cleansing, purification, and elimination is *absolutely accurate* in its interpretation.

➻ *Figure 3.7* confirms this because the place my DreamSelf lives in the third dimension is, again, within the slower vibrating energy of its three-dimensional Self, which is me and my everyday life.

➻ In saying that, my DreamSelf's "bathroom" is my own three-dimensional power and ability to cleanse, purify, and eliminate within my everyday physical self and my life.

I now want you to go to your Dreamtime Dream Dictionary (where you are writing down the dream symbol interpretations we've been interpreting) and write down the third dream symbol we have just interpreted and figured out, the dream symbol of a "bathroom." Next to it, put the = sign and write the Dreamtime interpretation for the dream symbol of a "bathroom." Your Dreamtime Dream Dictionary should look like *figure 3.8* below.

Figure 3.8

My Dreamtime Dream Dictionary

House =   **A communication from my DreamSelf regarding me, my physical body and my everyday life.**

Living Room =   **A communication from my DreamSelf regarding information that is going on within the "center" of myself and my life.**

Bathroom =   **A communication from my DreamSelf regarding my three-dimensional power and ability within to be a place of cleansing, purification, and elimination for my physical Self and life.**

Figure 3.7

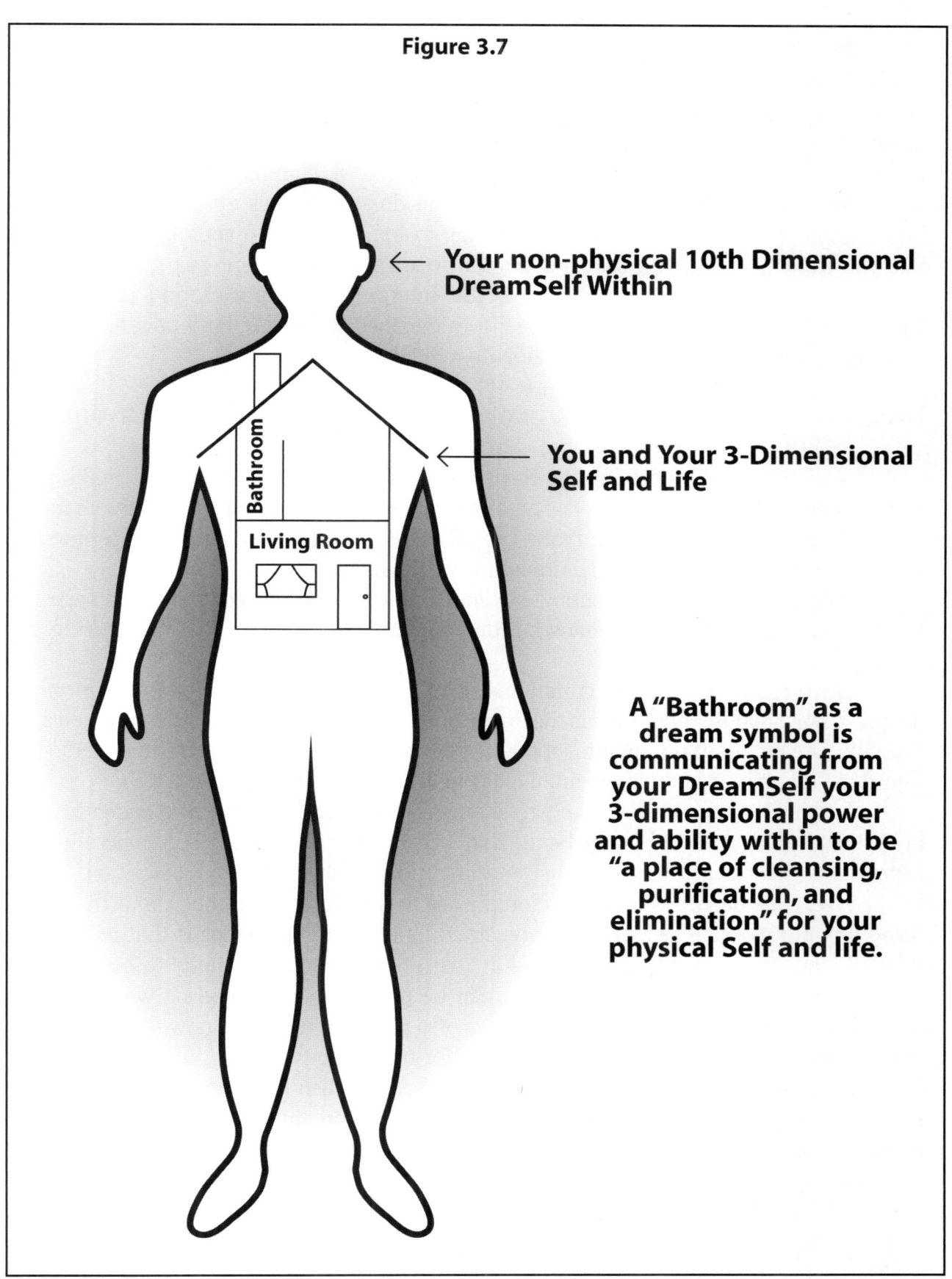

← Your non-physical 10th Dimensional DreamSelf Within

Bathroom

Living Room

← You and Your 3-Dimensional Self and Life

A "Bathroom" as a dream symbol is communicating from your DreamSelf your 3-dimensional power and ability within to be "a place of cleansing, purification, and elimination" for your physical Self and life.

With the dream symbol of a bathroom of a house, my DreamSelf is communicating *information* to me regarding my three-dimensional power and ability to cleanse, purify, and eliminate within my everyday Self and my life. Now is the bathroom in the dream orderly and spotless (= you feeling vital and fresh). Or is the toilet plugged and the bathtub in need of cleaning (= you not cleaning up and/or eliminating in your life).

As we discussed earlier, the details of your dream symbols give you more specific information of what your DreamSelf is trying to communicate to you. And don't worry that you will miss something attached to your dream symbol. You are smart, intuitive, and your DreamSelf Within knows this! As you interpret your dreams and practice the Dreamtime Method, it will become easier to remember and understand how to interpret the specific details surrounding your dream symbols.

Dreamtime Dream Interpretation of a "Man" or "Men" in Your Dreams

Now that you are getting the flavor of how your DreamSelf Within thinks as it creates your dream symbols, let's do something different. Let's stay in the bathroom in our dreamed dream. As I am in the bathroom of the house in my dream, I glance into the mirror. Reflected back to me is the dream symbol image of a "man."

(Reader, use a blank Dreamtime Method Template page located starting on page 135 to fill out as we interpret the following dream symbol of a "man" or "men" using the Dreamtime Method).

Universally, most of us commonly see and observe *male and female figures* of people in our dreams. What then is the image of a "male figure" or a "man" communicated from my DreamSelf in my dream supposed to mean? Let's use the Dreamtime Method to figure out the universal dream symbol of a "man" or "men" in our dream.

I start by taking the normal physical, three-dimensional definition and understanding of "a man" which is "a human being that in our everyday world one generally and generically associates with physical strength, 'action,' or the ability to 'take action.' "

Everyone has heard the common phrase at one time or another about the world being a man's world. The "unsaid" understanding of this phrase means that men get to take all "the action" in life, or that it is a "man's world" when action is to be had! The universal understanding of a man then can be understood as someone who "acts" or "takes action" in life. The everyday definition of a man (or men) I will now use to interpret this dream symbol is "the ability within to act or take action" in life.

With the dream symbol of a man in my dream, I then think of its meaning as my DreamSelf Within *thinks* of it, which is to interpret the dream symbol of the "man" as a three-dimensional "aspect, power, and ability" of my own everyday physical energy that I now possess from within.

As I think of myself as *being* the energy of a three-dimensional, physical "man" and then imagine myself as now being "the ability to act and take action within life," the interpretation that I get from "thinking" as my DreamSelf Within does, is that my DreamSelf is communicating information to me regarding my own three-dimensional ability "to act and take action" within my everyday Self and my life.

I now want you to look at *figure 3.9*. Illustrated in *figure 3.9* is the form of my 10th Dimensional DreamSelf. As you have seen from our previous illustrations, just outside the outline of the form is the faster vibrating non-physical energy of my 10th dimensional Self. As my DreamSelf's inner energy slows down in vibration and becomes the third-dimension as viewed within the outline of the form, my DreamSelf looks at all energy of the third dimension as my (and its) physical energy, which it is.

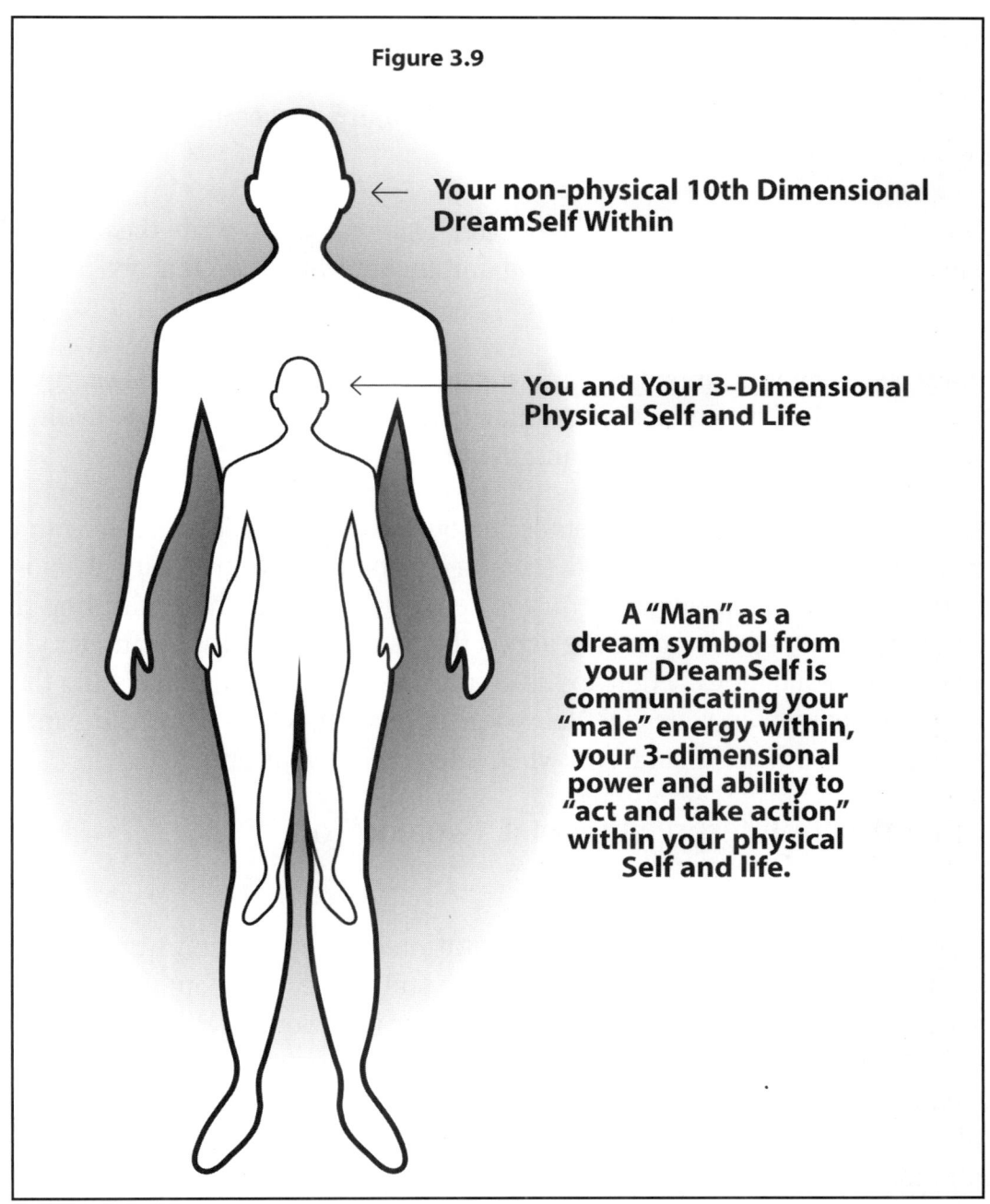

Figure 3.9

← **Your non-physical 10th Dimensional DreamSelf Within**

← **You and Your 3-Dimensional Physical Self and Life**

A "Man" as a dream symbol from your DreamSelf is communicating your "male" energy within, your 3-dimensional power and ability to "act and take action" within your physical Self and life.

In desiring to communicate to me that I now need to take some action in my three-dimensional life (my inner ability to act), my DreamSelf creates the dream symbol of a man in my dream. My DreamSelf does this because the generic, everyday definition that we associate with a "man" is *an ability to act or take action* in life. My DreamSelf knows that I, being its "three-dimensional Self," will associate this meaning for the dream symbol of a *man* and intuitively understand what it is trying to say to me.

⇝ In understanding this, the illustration in *figure 3.9* is absolutely correct and accurate in its interpretation!

⇝ And, with the dream symbol of a "man," my DreamSelf is communicating to me in my dream that it wants to tell me information regarding my own "male energy within" or my three-dimensional power and ability "to act and take action" within my everyday physical Self and life.

Now turn back to your Dreamtime Dream Dictionary and write the dream symbol of a "man or men." Next to this, put the Dreamtime interpretation that we just came up with:

Man or men = A communication from my DreamSelf regarding my "male energy" within which is my three-dimensional ability "to act or take action" within my everyday physical Self and in life.

Now just what are the specific details surrounding the "man or men" in your dream? Is the man in your dream strong and forceful symbolizing your ability to move with strength in your three-dimensional life? Or is he walking on crutches indicating that you are now possibly crippled regarding the action that is going on within your everyday life? Are there several men taking "action' in the dream, interpreting/communicating that "a lot of action" is needed now in your life? Note these important details of your dream symbol of the man (men) and write them down when interpreting your dream.

Dreamtime Dream Interpretation of a "Woman" or "Women" in Your Dreams

Now that you understand the interpretation of the important universal dream symbol of a man, let's go on to imagine that I am still in the bathroom in my dream. But this time when I glance into the mirror, I see the image of a woman. What might the dream symbol of a "female" be communicating to me from my DreamSelf?

(Reader, use a blank Dreamtime Method Template page located starting on page 135 to fill out as we interpret the following dream symbol of a "woman" or "women" using the Dreamtime Method.)

Using the Dreamtime Method, I start by taking the normal physical, three-dimensional definition and understanding for a "woman." The normal, physical definition of a woman is "a human being that generally and generically in our everyday world we associate with the qualities of *receptivity, creativity, and intuition.*" We usually refer to a female as having "woman's intuition." Thus the everyday generic definition of a woman (or women) that I will use to interpret this common dream symbol is "receptivity, creativity, and intuition."

I then think of this meaning as my DreamSelf Within *thinks* of it, that the dream symbol of the "woman" is now a "physical aspect, power, and ability" of my own three-dimensional energy that comes from within.

As I think of myself as *being* the energy of a three-dimensional, physical "woman" and then imagine myself as now being "receptive, creative, and intuitive," the interpretation that I get from "thinking" as my DreamSelf Within *thinks* is that my DreamSelf is communicating information to me about my three-dimensional power and ability to be receptive, creative, and intuitive within my everyday physical Self and life.

Now look at *figure 3.10*. Illustrated in *figure 3.10* just outside the outline of the form is the faster vibrating non-physical energy of my 10th dimensional Self. As my DreamSelf's inner energy slows down in vibration and becomes the third dimension as viewed within the outline of the form, my DreamSelf accordingly perceives all of the energy of the third dimension as my (and its) physical energy, which it is.

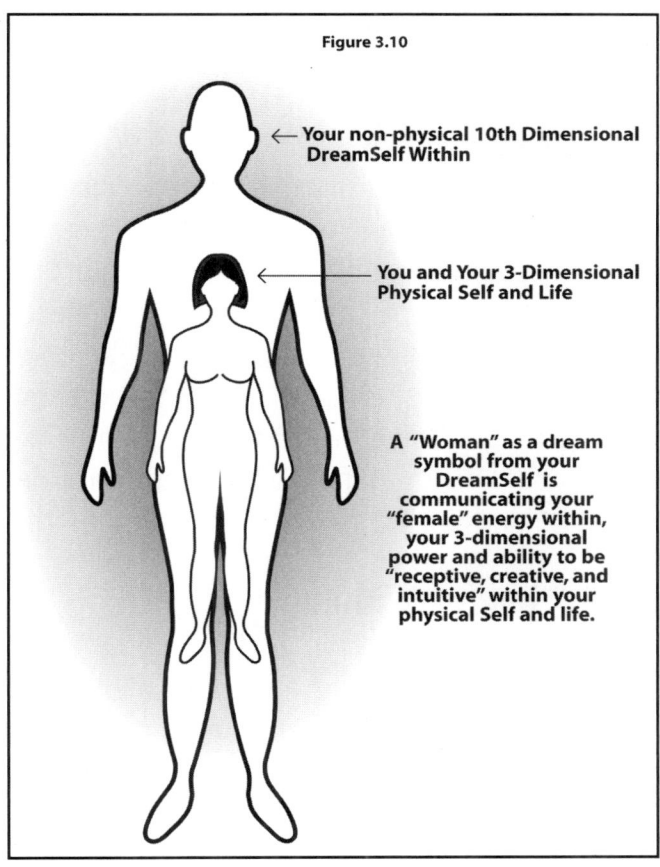

Figure 3.10

← **Your non-physical 10th Dimensional DreamSelf Within**

← **You and Your 3-Dimensional Physical Self and Life**

A "Woman" as a dream symbol from your DreamSelf is communicating your "female" energy within, your 3-dimensional power and ability to be "receptive, creative, and intuitive" within your physical Self and life.

In desiring to communicate to me that it wants me to address my receptivity, creativity, and intuition, my inner ability to *be* "female energy," my DreamSelf creates the dream symbol of a woman in my dream. My DreamSelf does this because the generic, everyday definition that we associate with a woman is receptivity, creativity, and intuition. My DreamSelf knows that I being its "three-dimensional Self" will associate this meaning for the dream symbol of a woman and intuitively understand what it is trying to say to me.

⟿ In understanding this, the illustration in *figure 3.10* is *absolutely correct and accurate* in its interpretation!

⟿ And, with the dream symbol of a "woman," my DreamSelf is communicating to me in my dream that it wants to tell me information regarding my three-dimensional power and ability to be receptive, creative, and intuitive within my physical self and in my life.

Now turn back to your Dreamtime Dream Dictionary and at this time write the dream symbol of a "woman or women." Next to it put the Dreamtime interpretation that we have just come up with which is:

Woman or women = A communication from my DreamSelf regarding my "female energy" within, which is my three-dimensional power and ability to be receptive, creative, and intuitive within my physical Self and my life.

Now is the woman in your dream attractive and popular? With these details, your DreamSelf is communicating to you that you now have a positive attitude (attractive, popular) regarding your talents, abilities, and creativity (= your female energy within). Or is the woman in your dream "unkempt," indicating that you need to clean up the image you now have regarding your creativity within. Are there a lot of women in your dream, indicating that you have "multitudinous" creativity going on within your life? Once again, as you interpret your dream symbol of a woman or women in your dream, make sure when writing your dream symbol down to include the important details surrounding this common dream symbol.

Your "Male and Female" Energy Within

As I said earlier, the dream symbols of a man (or men) and a woman (or women) are universally common in dreams. A point I want you to understand is that whether you are a male or a female in waking reality, within your total and whole multi-dimensional Self, you possess both "male and female" energy.

✓ A dream symbol of a man as a communication from your DreamSelf always represents, *whether you are male or female* dreaming of it, your "male energy" within or "your ability to act" in your life.

✓ A dream symbol of a woman communicated from your DreamSelf always represents, *whether you are male or female* dreaming of it, your "female energy" within or your ability to be "receptive, creative, and intuitive" in your life.

✓ Remember, these two energies added together make you total, whole, and are *who you are*. You will see your "male" and "female" energy clearly presented to you as dream communications from your DreamSelf with the figure(s) of a man (or men) and a woman (or women) in your dreams.

Interpreting the Meaning of "Other People" Accurately in Your Dreams

Now that you have the formula for the Dreamtime Method down for interpreting your dream symbols from our previous examples, I will bring up a common question people ask when interpreting their dreams: *"What does it mean when I dream of other people that I know in my everyday life?"* In considering this question, I'll answer it by using the Dreamtime Method. I'll do this by having you imagine now that I am stepping out of the dream house in my dream and, as I do, I see a female friend who I know in my everyday living standing on the street.

(Reader, use a blank Dreamtime Method Template page located starting on page 135 to fill out as we interpret the following dream symbol of a "female friend" using the Dreamtime Method).

In interpreting the above dream symbol of a "female friend" who I know in my waking reality, from previously using the Dreamtime Method to interpret the dream symbol of a woman, I have understood this symbol to represent my own "female energy within" or my inner receptivity, creativity (talents and abilities), and intuition. So to begin with, because of the fact that my friend is "female," I'll start interpreting this dream symbol with the understanding that my DreamSelf wants to communicate information to me regarding my own "female energy" within or *my own* inner receptivity, creativity, and intuition.

As I continue to use the Dreamtime Method to understand what may specifically be communicated to me by my female friend in my dream, I start by taking the "three-dimensional definition" I have of my friend. To do this, I start by thinking about what, in my everyday living, I feel and associate with her and her own talents, abilities, and creativity (her female energy within). As I define my friend's abilities, I feel that she is "very talented" and "highly successful" in her everyday life and career.

I then think of this meaning/understanding as my DreamSelf Within *thinks* of it, which is as though the dream symbol of my "female friend" (and what I associate with her) is now a "physical aspect, power, and ability" of my own (female) energy that I possess from within.

As I think of myself being the energy of my three-dimensional, physical "female friend" and imagine myself as now being "very successful with *my own* talents and abilities" (as she is), the interpretation that I get from "thinking" as my DreamSelf does is that with the dream symbol of my "female friend," my DreamSelf is communicating information to me about *my own creativity* which I am to understand is exactly *how* I feel about my friend's creativity!

This understanding means that with the dream symbol of my female friend, my DreamSelf is communicating information to me about whatever it is that I feel about her (= successful and talented) that this is how I should now be looking and understanding *my own creativity within* (my own female energy within).

I now want you to look at *figure 3.11*. Illustrated within *figure 3.11* along the outside outline of the form (as you already know!) is the faster vibrating non-physical energy of my 10th dimensional Self. As my DreamSelf's inner energy slows down in vibration and becomes the third dimension as viewed within the outline of the form, my DreamSelf accordingly perceives all of the energy of the third dimension as my (and its) everyday physical energy. In looking at the third dimension in this multi-dimensional way, my DreamSelf, in wanting to let me know that I should be looking at *my inner creativity* as though *I am talented and successful*, creates the dream symbol of my female friend.

The reason that my DreamSelf does this is because it knows that I, as its three-dimensional Self, will automatically associate and intuit my female friend's "female energy" with my own "female energy" (my inner creativity) and her "being successful" with myself "being successful."

→ In understanding this, the illustration in *figure 3.11* is absolutely correct and accurate in its interpretation!

→ And, with the dream symbol of my female friend, my DreamSelf is communicating in my dream that it wants to me to perceive my creativity and talents just as I do my friend's, which is of great value!

Now that we have interpreted the meaning of a "female friend" who you know from your everyday living using the Dreamtime Method, remember to go to your Dreamtime Dream Dictionary page and write this dream symbol down. Write your female friend's name and, next to it, write the Dreamtime interpretation that we have just come up with:

Figure 3.11

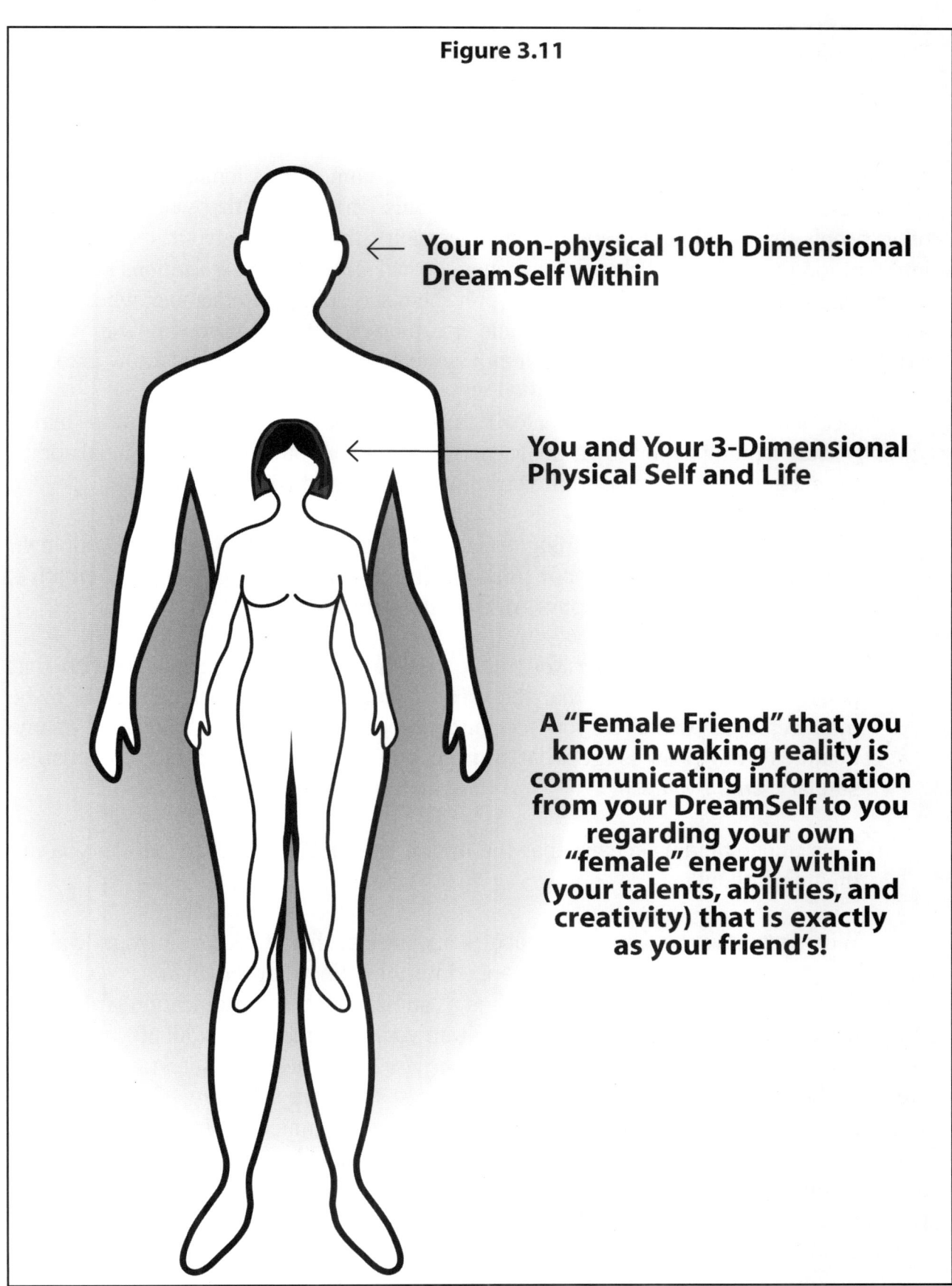

← Your non-physical 10th Dimensional DreamSelf Within

← You and Your 3-Dimensional Physical Self and Life

A "Female Friend" that you know in waking reality is communicating information from your DreamSelf to you regarding your own "female" energy within (your talents, abilities, and creativity) that is exactly as your friend's!

Female friend (name) = A communication from my DreamSelf regarding how I should be perceiving my own talents, abilities, and creativity (my female energy) that is exactly as my friend's.

Now every time in future dreams when you dream of this female friend, you will always associate this interpretation with her. This also then means that when dreaming of other people that you know from your waking reality, the only time your specific dream interpretation meaning will change is when your own *feelings and associations about that person* changes and you should then interpret them accordingly! Remember, whether you are a man dreaming of a female or a female dreaming of a man that you know in waking reality, the way that you interpret the dream symbol of someone that you know is to:

✓ Decide if they are male or female. If the person you are dreaming about is "male," you are looking at your own "male energy" within or your three-dimensional ability to "act and take action" within your physical Self and your life.

✓ If the person you are dreaming about is "female," you are looking at your own "female energy" within or your three-dimensional ability to be "receptive, creative, and intuitive" within your physical Self and your life.

✓ You then add in whatever you think, feel, and associate specifically with that person. Then understand that the dream symbol of the "other person" is to be interpreted as whatever you feel and associate with them, that those "same qualities" they possess are what you are, and should be seeing that you possess similary *within yourself*.

✓ This understanding means that the dream is about you not the person you are dreaming about!

When you have the dream symbol of someone else that you know in your "waking reality" in your dream, it's easy to get trapped into thinking that *the dream is about him or her*. But your dream and dream energy is a "supernatural communication" from your own inner DreamSelf that originates from within you! That means that all of your dream symbols mirror *your energy within, not someone else's!* You need to understand that your dream and its content is *about you and not the person you are dreaming about!*

In the example of our female friend above, the communication from my DreamSelf was saying that I needed to look at my creativity as "valuable and successful." But what if you dreamed of a male friend, for example, who you know in your everyday living that you consider a "deadbeat" type of guy? In this instance, your dream symbol of the deadbeat male person is communicating from your DreamSelf:

→ Your male energy within (he in the dream being male) which is symbolizing and representing (=) your ability to act and take action within your Self and your life.

→ He being a "deadbeat type" in waking reality is suggesting that you are now exhibiting (and mirroring) *the deadbeat traits exactly like the man in your dream* regarding your ability "to act and take action" within your everyday Self and life.

The above understanding provides another example of how you are to interpret "other people" that you know in everyday living when you dream of them. The "formula" for interpreting "other people" that you see in your dream holds true whether you are dreaming of celebrities, famous people, parents, your kids, or whomever from your three-dimensional life. Whatever you feel, associate, and think about the other people in your dream is what you *are seeing that is similarly within yourself!*

Remember, the reason your DreamSelf uses other people that you know from waking reality as dream symbols to communicate to you is that your 10th-dimensional DreamSelf looks at all physical energy of the third dimension as its own (slowed down) physical energy which multi-dimensionally, it is! This means that all energies of the third dimension are really created aspects of you and that you are just learning this multi-dimensional fact by using the Dreamtime Method to interpret your dreams! Interpreting "other people" seems to be one of the most difficult aspects for people to understand when they first start interpreting their dreams. When you interpret "other people" in your dream as though they are "mirroring the energy of yourself within" (which they are!), this will become easier and easier for you to understand.

The Absolute Accuracy of the Dreamtime Method of Interpreting Your Dreams

After interpreting a variety of common dream symbols as we have done above, I want you to understand that there is not one dream symbol that you cannot "figure out" accurately when using the Dreamtime Method to interpret your dream symbols!

To summarize the Dreamtime Method:

→ You start by taking the normal three-dimensional definition and understanding for the dream symbol.

→ You then think of that understanding as your DreamSelf Within does, which is that you *are* the actual physical, three-dimensional definition/energy of your dream symbol. By "thinking" in this way, you interpret your dream symbol's definition and understanding as your DreamSelf Within does, which is as though your dream symbol's meaning is now a "physical aspect, power, and ability" that you now three-dimensionally have and possess from within.

➻ As you think in this way, the information you receive gives you an absolutely accurate interpretation of your dream symbol.

Your DreamSelf *thinks* that it is the "creator" of your life, which it is! So for you to "think" as your DreamSelf Within to accurately interpret your dream symbol communication, you must imagine yourself as being the "creator" of your dream.

Thus to interpret your dream symbol's meaning accurately, you need to look at each dream symbol's definition/understanding as being a "created aspect" of your own three-dimensional energy/power that you now have and possess from within. The information that you then receive as you think in this way gives you an accurate interpretation of your dream symbol, which mirrors (and creates) what is currently going on within you and your three-dimensional life!

A good, fun exercise to do to practice "multi-dimensional thinking" as your DreamSelf Within thinks is to, *in your everyday waking reality*, look at each physical aspect of energy that surrounds you (your pet, your car, your vacuum, your friend, your spouse, etc.) as though you created it. Taking the above example of your physical household "vacuum," this three-dimensional object would be *multi-dimensionally* representing your ability within to clean up the dirt and debris covering the foundation (= the floor) of your physical Self and your life (= your house). Your pet dog would be representing your ability within to *faithful and loyal* (= the dog) to yourself plus whatever you feel and associate with it.

Try to think of what the different three-dimensional energies that surround you in your everyday life may be representing and symbolizing as though they are all now "created aspects" of yourself within similar to when you may have dreamed them in a dream. If you do this fun multi-dimensional exercise in your everyday "thinking," it will give you the gist of how your DreamSelf is "thinking" as it communicates your dreams symbols to you, helping you to learn and use the Dreamtime Method to get the most accurate information and interpretations from your dreams.

What's Ahead

Now that you understand how to interpret each of your dream symbols accurately by using the Dreamtime Method and thinking as your DreamSelf Within does, we'll move on to Chapter Four.

In Chapter Four, I'll start by teaching you how to keep a Dream Journal. A Dream Journal is fun, easy to do and writing down your dreams will help you remember them! You will then learn specifically how to take your fully written out dream from your dream journal and interpret it sentence by sentence using the Dreamtime Method. You may ask why it is important to learn to interpret your dream sentence by sentence? From my experience when I first began writing out my dreams to be interpreted, I would sometimes panic at the sheer size of what I had written down and wonder where do I begin? I found myself after writing my recalled dream down, being somewhat overwhelmed at my dream, not really knowing where to begin to start to interpret it.

When learning the Dreamtime Method to interpret your dreams, you will never get overwhelmed, confused or "not know" *where* to begin to interpret them. The reason being is with the Dreamtime Method, you will learn to start interpreting your dream with the first dream symbol from the first sentence of your written down dream, going on from there, in an ordered and logical way!

I'll see you in Chapter Four!

Learning to Keep a Dream Journal And Interpreting Your Written Dream Using the Dreamtime Method

Keeping a Dream Journal

Now that you have easily learned how to interpret each of your individual dream symbols using the Dreamtime Method, this is an excellent time to talk about keeping a Dream Journal. If you are serious about learning to interpret your dreams to understand what your inner DreamSelf is saying to you, *you must keep a Dream Journal* of your dreams. Dream Journals are important for many reasons:

✓Keeping a Dream Journal *guarantees* that you will remember and recall your dreams if you are having the problem of not remembering them! It is an absolute sure-fired way of remembering your dreams and bringing lots more of your dream information to you consciously as you wake up. Writing even one or two of your dream symbols down that you can remember grounds your dream energy into the third-dimension, allowing you to recall your future dreams more clearly and abundantly. (More about how to remember your dreams is covered in Chapter 7.)

✓Writing your dream down in your journal will aid you in making your dream energy, which is creating your life, manifest and come about more quickly. It speeds up your life. The pedal will be to the metal within you! If you have specific goals you want to accomplish or whatever it is you want to create, you will accelerate this within your life.

✓As you learn to interpret your dreams, writing your dream down allows you to interpret your dream immediately; and if you do not have time to interpret it at that time, you can return to your written dream later in the day, where it will be fully recorded and waiting for you.

Your Dream Journal can be any notebook. Keep it by your bedside. If you wake up in the middle of the night and remember a dream, jot down a few symbols. They will trigger the memory of your dream to then be written out more fully in the morning. I know we are all busy people, but writing your dreams down is important *because they are creating your life*!

Over the years, I have developed a unique, but easy way to record dreams. My Dreamtime Dream Journal approach uses specific headings for the daily recording of your dreams. *Figure 4.1* has a sample page from my Dream Journal showing the headings and format. For example, I would use one page for one dream and if I had two or three dreams I remembered from one night, I would accordingly use additional Dream Journal pages from my journal so each dream would be recorded on its own specific Dream Journal page. That means that you don't have to cram all your dreams or *dreamlettes* (which are multiple dream sequences) from the same night on one Dream Journal page.

In this book, I have included multiple Dreamtime Dream Journal pages with the above headings in place for you to start to record your dreams as you learn to interpret them using the Dreamtime Method. You can find them starting on page 145, so check them out. You can also write these same headings in your own Dream Journal if you choose. I have found these headings to be most helpful to myself and others for the recording of dreams, *because they remind you* that your dreams come from an absolutely supernatural part of yourself within, your unique multi-dimensional DreamSelf Within!

As you can see in *figure 4.1.*, I start each page of my Dream Journal by dating the day I had the dream. If I were writing the dream down in the morning, I would write down the previous day's date, since that is when I had the dream. For example, if I were writing the dream on the 12th day of the month, I would date the dream when writing it in my Dream Journal as the 11th.

I then act as though I am writing a letter to myself, since the dream is a communication from my DreamSelf Within. This means that your dream really is a letter, a message and communication from supernatural you to everyday you! So, after I date the Dream Journal page, I then write the following at the top of the page below the date.

Dear Terri, (Insert your own name.)

The next step is to write your dream down as fully as you can remember it in exactly the order your dream occurred. It is important to write down your dream in the exact sequence it occurred because that is how you are going to interpret each of your dream symbols using the Dreamtime Method. As you are writing the dream out, if you then remember something that happened in a different sequence, just go back to when and where it occurred in the dream and include it.

Figure 4.1

Dreamtime Dream Journal

Date:

Dear_____,

(Write your dream out as you remember it in the exact order that events occurred here.)

My DreamSelf says that within my thinking and thoughts creating my now . . .

(Use the Dreamtime method to interpret your dream symbols here.)

What happened that day:

(Write what happened the day after you had this dream to show yourself how your dreams and dream symbols are creating your next physical day).

After your dream is written out, leave a "space" following it for the actual interpretation. If you had two or three dream sequences or dreamlettes, each one should go on its own page as noted above. Try to write your dream sequences on the pages in the order that you dreamed them.

Note that as I start out my interpretation, I always write the following sentence:
"My DreamSelf says that within my thinking and thoughts creating my now . . ."

So you'll also want to write that sentence at the top of the space you're leaving for writing out the interpretation. I recommend that you should get into the *good habit* of using this sentence every time to start out your dream interpretation. I do it myself for two reasons:

✓ To remind myself that my dream is coming from my "all-knowing and unlimited inner guidance," my DreamSelf Within.

✓ For me to remember (in case I had forgotten) that *my actual thinking and thoughts* are creating my now! Writing the above sentence out before I interpret my dream is a great way to remember this. You'll be surprised at how, as you interpret your dreams, this *reminder sentence* written out will get your attention to recall where *within you* your dreams are coming from and how you, as a multi-dimensional Being, are creating your three-dimensional Self and life.

"What Happened That Day"

After leaving room for the actual interpretation, near the bottom of the page you may write another heading; this heading is purely optional, but *as a dream expert, I recommend it!* I write out: "What happened that day." This line is already written out for you on the dream journal form.

If I have time the day after I have interpreted a dream to go back to the previous day's dream interpretation in my journal, in the space where I have written: "What happened that day," I give a short synopsis of what *did happen* in that previous day. The reason I do this and feel it would be important for you to go back and do this, especially when you are first learning how to interpret your dreams, is that this allows you to actually see *how* your dream symbols, as multi-dimensional energy, create by drawing in similar energy to you which is your next three-dimensional, physical day.

An example of going back and writing down what happened in my Dream Journal the day after I had interpreted a dream can be understood this way. Say I had a dream that I was riding a bicycle. The next day I write this dream down in my Dream Journal.

Using the Dreamtime Method to interpret this dream (where I think/interpret each of my dream symbols as though each is a physical aspect and ability that I now possess from within), I start by using the normal everyday definition of a bicycle, which is a "two-wheeled vehicle that requires balance to ride."

I then think of that definition/understanding as my DreamSelf Within *thinks* of it, which is as though the dream symbol of the bicycle is now a physical aspect, power and ability of my own everyday three-dimensional energy within.

As I think of myself being the physical energy of the three-dimensional bicycle, the interpretation that I get from *thinking* as my DreamSelf Within does is that for the dream symbol of a bicycle, my DreamSelf wants to communicate information to me about my own inner ability to move (the bicycle being a vehicle) through my life with balance (a bicycle requiring balance to ride). This means that using the Dreamtime Method, my dream symbol of riding a bicycle from my DreamSelf interprets/communicates to mean: my own inner ability to move along in my everyday living in a "balanced" way.

Now imagine that in my waking reality, the day after dreaming of the bicycle, I had a very busy day scheduled. But then, all of a sudden, some of my appointments cancelled, which freed me up to take a walk in the park. As I did this, I then felt more relaxed and in turn more balanced than if I had just done my usual workday.

The next morning, as I am writing my dream down in my Dream Journal, I go back to the previous day's dream of riding the bicycle. At the end of that dream interpretation, I had written the heading, "What happened that day." And now next to it I write: I was able to not just work yesterday, as some appointments cancelled. I then went to the park where I had a great time; I relaxed and was able to bring some much-needed balance into my day and life.

To start, interpreting my dream using the Dreamtime Method *consciously gave me* the information that I needed to bring some balance in my life. Then during my day, when my appointments cancelled, my interpreted dream information of that morning reminded me that instead of scheduling more appointments and making myself more harried and out of balance (my old energy scenario), I might take a walk in the park which I did, bringing some harmony and balance into my day.

Then, by going back and writing out what *did happen* in my previous day the next day, I was able to *clearly see and understand* the connection between my *dream symbol energy* of the bicycle in my dream with my three-dimensional ability to take action to create some much needed balance in my life. The dream symbol of the bicycle was the 10th dimensional dream energy that created the three-dimensional circumstances for me to make the *conscious choice* to take the walk in the park allowing (manifesting) balance in my day.

And, as we discussed in Chapters Two and Three, your dream energy as the thinking and thoughts of your 10th dimensional DreamSelf, not only *tells* and gives you knowing information, but *creates!* Your dreams not only *tell* you what's going on in your life, but as your own "multi-dimensional energy" from within attract into your next day and days after dreaming your dream, similar three-dimensional (physical energy) to provide the solution for whatever your dream is addressing. It is in this way that your dreams *create* your everyday, three-dimensional reality.

Remember, as you master the Dreamtime Method, the *knowing understandings* of your dream symbols will become *automatic* within you and your everyday life as I have told you previously. This process will occur quickly as you interpret your dreams using the Dreamtime Method. But initially as you are learning how to interpret your dreams, going back to your previous day's dream and writing out "what did happen that day" will accelerate you to seeing and becoming aware of how your dreams are creating your everyday three-dimensional life.

Your Personal Dream Journal

The best time to write down your dreams is in the morning as soon as you awaken. Why? Because you are *closest* to your multi-dimensional DreamSelf of your inner Dreamtime just after sleeping and dreaming. You know how when you wake up in the morning and *feel as though you have been in another reality or someplace else?* You have been; you've been in the multi-dimensions of your Dreamtime Within!

As you make regular entries into your Dream Journal, your Dream Journal will become *addicting!* You are going to see some beautiful things in your dreams. Once you learn what your dreams mean and realize that they come from a place *within* you that is infinitely intelligent and all knowing, you'll want to know more and more, I guarantee it! Your dreams, as your DreamSelf's vision for you, are fun and exciting—especially when you see them written down and recorded in your own personal Dream Journal.

Interpreting Your Dream Sentences Using the Dreamtime Method

Above in this chapter, when I spoke of keeping a Dream Journal, I said to write your dream down in the exact order that events occurred in your dream. The reason that I instructed you to do this is because that is how I will now teach you to interpret your dream symbols from your written dream sentences. Remember, starting on page 145 of this book, I have created Dreamtime Dream Journal pages with headings already in place for you to write out your dreams. You may want to go to one of those pages now to write out this "sample dream sentence" as an example of how to interpret your own written down dream's sentences using the Dreamtime Method. Also, in the following dream sentences, I will be using the Dreamtime Method Template form that we used in Chapter Three to interpret each dream symbol using the Dreamtime Method. I have blank Dreamtime Method Template forms for you to use starting on page 135 of this book as you continue to learn and use the Dreamtime Method.

I begin my Dream Journal by writing the date of my dream. I then write my dream out as fully as I can remember in the order that events occurred in my dream. I will now start with my first dream sentence which is the following:

1/10/2010

Dear Terri,

I dreamed I saw a man.

In interpreting this dream sentence, I next write:

My DreamSelf says that within my thinking and thoughts creating my now . . .

As I explained above when writing your dream down in your dream journal, writing this sentence out is purely optional, but I recommend it! The reason I recommend this when interpreting your own dreams is to remind you of where from within you your dream energy is originating (your DreamSelf Within) and that your thinking and thoughts are attracting to you the energy that is creating your everyday three-dimensional Self and life.

To interpret the above dream sentence, I start with the first words that I dreamed and then wrote which are:

I dreamed.

As you write out your dream communication with the words "I dreamed," this dream phrase will always "generically interpret" to mean that your dream is going on "within your own Self and life right now." The words "I dreamed" are always to be understood and interpreted as something that is going on or happening within you and your life right now. I usually start my dream interpretation with the words "I dreamed," interpreting them to mean: "within myself" or "within Self."

I dreamed = Within myself, within Self

The next word to be interpreted from our dream sentence is the word "saw." To interpret "verbs" from your dream, you would use the Dreamtime Method just as you have learned in Chapter Three. You will start by taking the normal, everyday definition of the verb. The normal physical, three-dimensional definition and understanding of the verb "saw" could be thought of as: "my ability within 'to see,' I am now 'seeing' or 'seeing within.'"

I then think of this definition meaning how my DreamSelf Within thinks of it, as though the dream symbol/verb of "seeing" is now a "physical aspect and ability" of my own three-dimensional energy that comes from within.

As I think of my own three-dimensional ability to "see" and imagine myself now doing the action of "seeing within," the interpretation that I get from "thinking" as my

DreamSelf Within does is that with the dream symbol/verb of "saw" (seeing), my DreamSelf wants to communicate information to me about my inner ability "to see" within my own three-dimensional Self and my life. That means that using the Dreamtime Method, the dream symbol/verb "saw" interprets to mean: "my own inner ability to 'to see' within myself and my three-dimensional life."

I dreamed (within myself right now), I saw (am seeing)

In Chapter Three, you have already learned, by using the Dreamtime Method, that the dream symbol interpretation of a "man" is: "my (your) ability to act and take action." So I'll now use that correct understanding.

man = my ability to act and take action

I will now add all of our above Dreamtime dream interpretations together to get a "complete thought" of what my DreamSelf Within is communicating to me in the above dream sentence.
Our dream sentence interprets to mean:

I dreamed (within myself and my life right now) I saw (I am seeing) a man
(my ability to act and take action).

This dream sentence using the Dreamtime Method without the dream symbols added in then interprets to mean:

Within myself and my life right now, I am seeing my own ability to act and
take action in my life.

As you can see in this dream sentence example:

✓ I wrote the dream sentence out as I dreamed it. ("I dreamed I saw a man.") Then starting with the first dream symbol, I used the Dreamtime Method to interpret the specific dream symbol.

✓ In parenthesis after each dream symbol I interpreted, I wrote the Dreamtime interpretation that I obtained.

✓ I then added those interpretations together to give myself the "whole thought" from the communication being given to me from my DreamSelf . . . which also gave me an absolutely accurate interpretation of my dream sentence.

As you can also see from the above example, by adding the dream interpretations/meanings together, you—being the person interpreting your dream—will be able to "intuit" how your dream meaning and interpretation relates to your life. With the above interpreted dream communication that *in my life right now, I can see my ability to act*, possibly I had been thinking of making "a change" in my everyday living situation. This subsequent dream and its message confirmed that to me "consciously," while also providing me the ability to attract in the three-dimensional energy that I needed to make "a change."

I have found that most of the time the dream interpretation people get when using the Dreamtime Method is something they already "know" because their dreams and the dream state mirrors (and is creating) their everyday three-dimensional lives! The key when interpreting your dream symbols using the Dreamtime Method is to keep in mind that your dream symbols, as the "thoughts" of your all-knowing DreamSelf Within, not only tell and "relate," but also, as your own multi-dimensional energy within, assist you to create!

→ Remember, your dream symbols as a communication from your DreamSelf not only give you intelligent information and guidance for you and your life, but also, as your own inner 10th dimensional "light energy," attract in more and similar energy after dreaming them to provide the physical, three-dimensional way (energy) to accomplish whatever your dream is addressing.

Understanding this, in my above dream sentence example and its interpretation: "I am seeing my ability within to act in my life," after dreaming this dream I would (and should) look in my next day and days for the way(s) to be available to take some "new and different action" in my everyday life. By interpreting the dream and becoming "consciously aware" of the need for me to make a change in my life, this information gave me the advantage in the days following the dream to act and take some action on situations and events going on within my life that I may have otherwise ignored, not taken action on, or thought of as being "coincidental." In other words, by consciously interpreting my dream and making myself aware that I needed to make a change, my "taking action" brought in the energy of "change" for my three-dimensional Self and life.

The Ease of Interpreting Your Dream Symbols and Adding Them Together·

Now that you're seeing how easy it is to use the Dreamtime Method to interpret and add your individual dream symbol meanings together into a sentence, let's continue on with another dream sentence (example) from my written down dream.

The next sentence in my dream after "I saw a man" is:

The man was sweeping the floor.

I start by taking my first dream symbol, "man," and interpret it using our Dreamtime dream interpretation.

The man = my inner ability to act and take action in my life.

Next I take the dream symbol verb "was sweeping." Using the Dreamtime Method, I take the normal physical, three-dimensional definition and understanding of the verb "sweep." The three-dimensional definition of the verb "sweep" would be "to clean up" as if someone was "sweeping" with a broom.

I then think of this definition/meaning as my DreamSelf Within thinks of it, which is as though the dream symbol/verb of "sweeping" is now a "physical aspect and ability" of my own three-dimensional energy that comes from within.

As I think of my own three-dimensional ability to "sweep" and imagine myself now doing the action of "sweeping/cleaning up," the interpretation that I get from "thinking" as my DreamSelf Within does is that with the dream symbol/verb of "sweeping," my DreamSelf wants to communicate information to me about my own inner ability "to clean or sweep up" within my three-dimensional Self and life.

This means that using the Dreamtime Method, the dream symbol/verb "sweeping" interprets to mean: "my own inner ability to 'clean or sweep up' within my three-dimensional Self and life."

I now put this interpretation next to the word "was sweeping" in my dream sentence.

The man (my inner ability to act and take action in my life) was sweeping (my ability to clean or sweep up).

The next dream symbol/word to be interpreted in our dream sentence is: the "floor." Using the Dreamtime Method, I interpret the dream symbol of a "floor." The normal physical, three-dimensional definition of a floor is usually understood as the "foundation" of a house.

As I think of myself as being a three-dimensional "floor" and imagine myself as the "foundation" of a house, the interpretation that I get from "thinking" as my DreamSelf Within thinks is that with the dream symbol of a floor, my DreamSelf wants to communicate information to me about "the foundation" within me of my three-dimensional Self and my life (the house). Using the Dreamtime Method, the dream symbol of a floor then interprets to mean: the "foundation" of my physical Self and life.

I will now add these interpretations to my dream symbol sentence.

The man (my ability within to act and take action in my life) was sweeping (my ability to clean or sweep up) the floor (the foundation of myself and my life within).

Putting all of these dream interpretations together, my DreamSelf Within is communicating with this dream sentence:

Put some action (the man) into cleaning up (sweeping) the foundation of yourself and your life within (the floor).

As you can see with this dream sentence:

✓ You write your dream out in the order that events occurred and then use the Dreamtime Method to interpret each one of your dream symbols in that order.

✓ You then add your interpreted dream symbol meanings together where your finished interpretation then gives you the complete "thoughts" of communication of your DreamSelf Within from your dream

The Amazement of Interpreting Your Dreams Using the Dreamtime Method

Let's continue on now and add the two previous dreams sentences together to see what our DreamSelf Within is communicating as a "whole" thought in this dream so far.

My written dream = I dreamed I saw a man. The man swept the floor.

The Dreamtime interpretation is saying:

My DreamSelf says that within my thinking and thoughts which is creating my now . . .

I dreamed (within myself and my life right now) I saw a man (I am seeing the need to act and take action). The man (I need to put some action) was sweeping (into cleaning up) the floor (the foundation of myself and my life within).

Let's put these two dream sentences and their interpretations together without the dream symbols/words added in.

Within myself and my life right now, I am seeing the need to act and take action. I need to clean up the foundation of myself and my life within.

From these two simple dream sentences above that we just interpreted using the

Dreamtime Method, we have learned some very valuable information! If you had dreamed this dream, you would now know that there is action needed to be taken in your immediate, everyday life. And your dream interpretation has specifically told you *how to take this action*, which is by making a "clean sweep" (sweeping with the broom) of whatever it is that is now cluttering the foundation of your life (the floor).

➤ You received this "complete thought" of information and guidance from your DreamSelf by writing your dream symbol/sentences out in the order that they occurred in your dream.

➤ You then took each dream symbol in your dream sentence in that order and used the Dreamtime Method to interpret each one of them.

➤ You then added all of the dream interpretations together in the order they occurred, to give yourself a comprehensive and "accurate" interpretation of your dream.

I remember the amazement I felt (and still do) when I first started using my simple Dreamtime Method to interpret my dreams and got *accurate information* that matched *exactly what was happening* in my life! I wondered *where* this information was coming from and it made me want to know more and more about my dreams.

As you interpret your dreams, you will learn "more and more" from your inner DreamSelf which opens up the big door of the unlimited multi-dimensional you! It's very exciting and as you do the fun, easy Dreamtime Method of interpreting your dreams, because your dream energy is your own supernatural energy coming from within, it leads to a completely expanded and transformed everyday, three-dimensional you!

Interpreting Multiple Sentences Using the Dreamtime Method

Now that I have generated some excitement with how enlightening, fun, and easy it is to understand/interpret your dreams using the Dreamtime Method, let's add another dream sentence to our dream to see what else my DreamSelf may be communicating.

The next dream sentence I dreamed was that:

I was looking around in a store.

Our first dream symbol words are: "I was."

I was = within myself right now

The next words to be interpreted in our dream sentence are the verbs "looking around." Using the Dreamtime Method, you take the normal definition and understanding for the verb "looking around" which could be interpreted as "seeing within" or "looking around within."

I then think of this definition/meaning as my DreamSelf Within *thinks* of it, which makes the dream symbol/verb of "looking around" a "physical aspect and ability" of my own three-dimensional energy that comes from within.

As I think of my three-dimensional ability to "look around" and imagine myself now doing the action of "looking" within, the interpretation that I get from "thinking" as my DreamSelf Within thinks is that with the dream symbol/verb of "looking around," my DreamSelf wants to communicate information to me about my own inner ability "to see and look within" my three-dimensional Self and life. Using the Dreamtime Method, the dream symbol/verb "looking around" interprets to mean: "my own inner ability to look and/or 'see within' myself and my three-dimensional life."

I dreamed I was (within myself right now) looking around (seeing within).

The next word in our dream sentence is a "store." Using the Dreamtime Method to interpret the dream symbol of a "store," I take the normal definition of a store which could be thought of as "a place of supplies and resources that are needed for everyday living." I then think as my DreamSelf Within *thinks*, which is that the dream symbol of the "store" is now a "physical aspect" of my own three-dimensional energy that comes from within.

As I think of myself as being a three-dimensional "store" and imagine myself as a "place within of supplies and resources," the interpretation I get for the dream symbol of a store is that my DreamSelf is communicating information to me about my own "inner store" (of resources) within for my everyday three-dimensional Self and life. Using the Dreamtime Method, the dream symbol of a "store" interprets to mean: "the 'inner resources' of myself and life within."

store = the inner resources of myself and my life within

Now let's add this dream sentence to our two previously interpreted dream sentences in our dream:

My written Dream =

Dear Terri,

I dreamed I saw a man. The man swept the floor. I was looking around a store.

My Dreamtime interpretation is saying:

My DreamSelf says that within my thinking and thoughts creating my now . . .
I dreamed I saw a man. (Within myself and my life right now, I am seeing
the need to act and take action). The man swept the floor. (I need to put some
action into cleaning up the foundation of myself and my life within.) I was
looking around a store. (In doing this, I am seeing my inner resources.)

Without the dream symbols added in, here is the meaning/interpretation of my dream:

Within myself and my life right now, I am seeing the need to act and take
action. I need to clean up the foundation of myself and my life within. (In
doing this) I am seeing my inner resources.

With this dream, my DreamSelf is communicating to me that right now I need to take some action (put some energy into) cleaning up the foundation of my life. As I take this action, I will see my "inner store," the inner resources I possess for myself and my life.

From interpreting and then adding the third dream sentence to our dream, you can see how this dream is giving me further information for my life. Didn't I tell you that interpreting your dreams with the Dreamtime Method would be fun, easy, and *very informative!*

Attaining the Complete Thoughts of Communication from Your DreamSelf Within

Let's continue on in our dream and see what other information we can get from our DreamSelf with the next dream sentence of our written-down dream.

Following the above interpreted dream sentences—I dreamed I saw a man. The man swept the floor. I was looking around a store—the next dream sentence is:

Within the store was a beautiful crystal.

Using the Dreamtime Method, I now interpret the first dream symbol in the above dream sentence which is: "Within the store." Since we have just interpreted a store to mean "my inner resources," I will interpret this to mean: "Within my inner resources."

Within the store = Within my inner resources

The next dream symbol in our sentence is:

a beautiful crystal

Using the Dreamtime Method, I now interpret the dream symbol of a "beautiful crystal."

We all understand the descriptive adverb of beautiful to mean: "attractive, stunning, and valuable" so I will add this understanding as I use the Dreamtime Method to interpret the dream symbol of a "crystal."

I take the normal definition of a "crystal" which is defined as "a quartz rock that has the ability to focus and magnify energy." I then think as my DreamSelf Within *thinks*, which is that the meaning of the dream symbol of the crystal is now a "physical aspect" of my own three-dimensional energy that comes from within.

As I think of myself as being a three-dimensional crystal and imagine myself as having the ability to focus and magnify energy, the interpretation I get for the dream symbol of a "crystal" is that my DreamSelf is communicating information to me about my valuable ability to focus and magnify the energy of my three-dimensional Self and life. This means that using the Dreamtime Method, the dream symbol of a "beautiful crystal" interprets to mean: "my valuable ability to focus and magnify energy within myself and my everyday life."

a beautiful crystal = my valuable ability to focus and magnify energy within myself and my everyday life

Adding this interpretation to our above dream symbol sentence, I get the following:

Within the store (within my inner resources) was (is) a beautiful crystal (my valuable ability to focus and magnify energy within myself and my everyday life).

Without the dream symbols added in, the Dreamtime interpretation of the above dream sentence is:

Within my inner resources is my valuable ability to focus and magnify energy for myself and my everyday life.

I will now add this interpreted dream sentence to the rest of our dream.

My written Dream =

Dear Terri,

I dreamed I saw a man. The man swept the floor. I was looking around a store. In the store was a beautiful crystal.

The Dreamtime interpretation is saying:

My DreamSelf says that within my thinking and thoughts which is creating my now . . .

I dreamed I saw a man. (Within myself and my life right now, I am seeing the need to act and take action.) The man swept the floor. (I need to put some action into cleaning up the foundation of myself and my life within.) I was looking around a store. (In doing this, I am seeing my inner resources.) In the store was a beautiful crystal. (Within my inner resources is my valuable ability to focus and magnify energy for myself and my everyday life.)

Without the dream symbols, here is the meaning/interpretation of our dream so far.

Within myself and my life right now, I am seeing the need to act and take action. I need to clean up the foundation of myself and my life within. (In doing this) I am seeing my inner resources. Within my inner resources is my valuable ability to focus and magnify energy for creating (making things happen) within myself and my everyday life.

As you can see, when interpreting the above dream paragraph using the Dreamtime Method, I wrote my dream out as I dreamed it. I then started with the first dream symbol of the first sentence and used the Dreamtime Method to interpret it. I then worked on from there just as you will do, interpreting each of the dream symbols from the sentence. I then added those interpretations together to receive the complete thoughts and communications of information from my DreamSelf Within.

Interpreting Additional Sentences Using the Dreamtime Method

Let's add one more sentence to this dream paragraph to make sure you are getting the gist of how to interpret each of your dream symbols using the Dreamtime Method and then the direction of how to add them together.

The next sentence/sequence of our dream is:

I saw a female friend.

We just previously interpreted the dream symbol words, "I saw" in a prior dream sentence. You have probably already written these two dream symbol interpretations down in your "Dreamtime Dream Dictionary," so let's reference back and recall what they mean:

I = within me, saw = am seeing or seeing within.

I saw (I am seeing) a female friend.

The next dream symbol/words in our sentence are: a "female friend," which we previously interpreted in Chapter Three. To refresh your memory, using the Dreamtime Method, the dream symbol of a "female" is a communication from my (your) DreamSelf giving information about your own "female energy" within or your own inner talents, abilities, and creativity whether you are a male or female dreaming of it.

✓ Keep in mind here that whenever you are dreaming of someone that you "know" in waking, everyday reality, whatever you think and feel about him or her is really what you are looking at within yourself. The dream is giving you information about you, not the person(s) you are dreaming about.

✓ You should view the person you are dreaming about as though they are now a "created" aspect and ability of your own Self. They are mirroring or representing to you whatever you think and feel about them that is exactly how you should be looking at yourself.

I will use the understanding/association of my "female friend" from the above dream sentence to mean that I think of my "female friend" as someone who has done well with her creativity and in doing so is highly successful in her everyday career and life.

As I use the Dreamtime Method to interpret the dream symbol of my "female friend," I think of this meaning as my DreamSelf Within *thinks* of it, which is as though the dream symbol of my "female friend" is a "physical aspect, power, and ability" that I now possess within myself.

As I think of myself as *being* my "female friend" or that in reality I am now highly successful when using my talents and abilities, the interpretation that I get from "thinking" as my DreamSelf does is that my DreamSelf is communicating information to me about *my own inner creativity* which I should value just as I value my friend's.

female friend = my own inner creativity which is very valued

Putting the above dream interpretations together, I now come up with this "complete thought" from my DreamSelf:

I saw (I am seeing) a female friend (the use of my inner creativity as though it is of much value).

Without the dream symbols, this dream sentence interprets to mean:

I am seeing my inner creativity as though it is of great value.

I will now add this interpreted dream sentence to the rest of my dream.

My written Dream =

Dear Terri,

I dreamed I saw a man. The man swept the floor. I was looking around a store. In the store was a beautiful crystal. I then saw a female friend.

The Dreamtime interpretation is saying:

My DreamSelf says that within my thinking and thoughts creating my now . . . I dreamed I saw a man. (Within myself and my life right now, I am seeing the need to act and take action.) The man swept the floor. (I need to put some action into cleaning up the foundation of myself and my life within.) I was looking around a store. (In doing this, I am seeing my inner resources.) In the store was a beautiful crystal. (Within my inner resources is my valuable ability to focus and magnify energy for making things happen within myself and my everyday life.) I then saw a female friend. (I am now seeing my own creativity, my keen ability to focus energy for my life as though it is of great value.)

Without the dream symbols, here is the meaning/interpretation of my dream using the Dreamtime Method.

Within myself and my life right now, I am seeing the need to act and take action. I need to clean up the foundation (of how I think) of myself and my life within. (In doing this) I am seeing my inner resources. Within my inner resources is my valuable ability to focus and magnify energy for making things happen (manifest) within myself and my life. I am now seeing this extraordinary talent as though it is of great value for me and my everyday life.

From interpreting the above dream sentences of our dream paragraph using the Dreamtime Method, we have learned much regarding an important communication of information from my (your) DreamSelf! If this dream had been about your life, you would have been informed that right now there is action you need to take within yourself and your life. The action involves cleaning up the basic foundation of how you think and perceive yourself. As you do this, you will see your valuable inner resources as they really exist. One of those resources is your innate ability to focus and magnify your creative energy so that you can manifest (make happen) a successful and prosperous three-dimensional Self and life!

Your Dream Energy As Creative Energy

As we discussed earlier in this book, the dream symbol information attained from interpreting our above dream paragraph, as your *own* inner 10th dimensional light energy, not only tells (and relates information to you), but creates! After interpreting your dream using the Dreamtime Method and understanding your DreamSelf's communication of information to you, you would look in your next day or days after dreaming your dream for the three-dimensional energy to be present in your life to address whatever your dream symbol/communication is bringing up to you.

Taking the above interpreted dream information, after dreaming this dream, you would look for the opportunity to create change (symbolized by your dream symbol of the "man") by cleaning up your thinking and thoughts you have of yourself (the man sweeping the floor) to a more valuable perception of your inner worth (the beautiful crystal). In doing so, this would allow you to act on energy that presents itself within your three-dimensional Self and life to create a new start (dreaming of your female friend).

The tremendous advantage the Dreamtime Method gives you over someone who is not interpreting their dreams consciously is the *knowing ability* of when to act on three-dimensional energy when it presents itself into your life (the energy that is attracted to you by your dreamed dream symbols). This would be versus the common, everyday thinking that you are either just *lucky or unlucky* in life and the things happening to you are *coincidental*. And the best thing about "knowing" what your dreams mean consciously and connecting their understandings/energies to your three-dimensional Self and life is that it demonstrates to you that *you are the conscious creator* of your everyday Self and life. And this, dear Dreamers, is great *knowledge and power* to have in the third-dimension!

Most people in their waking reality recall their dreams as being illogical and silly with no real connection to their everyday three-dimensional Self and life. With the Dreamtime Method of understanding your dreams, *you are learning differently!* Our above "interpreted dream paragraph" gives you a good idea of how once you interpret your dream using the Dreamtime Method, your dreams and dream symbols transform into amazing guidance *chocked full* of information for you and your life! By using the Dreamtime Method to interpret your dreams, you are learning a consistent and directed method of interpretation which shows you that your dreams and their meanings are very logical, extremely ordered, and full of astounding information with actual transforming creative energy for you and your everyday physical life!

Let's Review

In summary for Chapter Four, as you can see from our dream symbol sentence examples above, when using the Dreamtime Method to determine the meaning of your dream symbols, your formula for interpreting will always be the same! This is true whether you have one dream symbol in your dream, are adding single sentences together, or are dealing with a dream paragraph, or additional dream paragraphs. The process will always be the same and it is to:

→ Start by writing your dream out in your Dream Journal in the exact sequence of events that occurred in your dream.

→ You then take each dream symbol in your dream sentence in that order and use the Dreamtime Method to interpret each one.

→ Lastly you add all of the Dreamtime dream interpretations from your dream sentences together in the order they occurred, which will give you the "complete thoughts" of what your DreamSelf Within is communicating to you. This gives you an absolutely "accurate" interpretation of your whole dream.

More Dreams Ahead

Now that you have a good foundation of how to use the Dreamtime Method to interpret your dream symbols and to add those dream symbols together to get the complete thoughts of your DreamSelf in your dream, we'll move on to Chapter Five.

In Chapter Five, for your continued learning, review, and interest, I have dreams listed that I received from people all around the world whose dreams I interpreted using the Dreamtime Method. These dreams contain common dream themes that we all see in our dreams such as: repeat dreams, nightmare dreams, sex dreams, etc. I will give you my general understanding of why these dream themes so commonly occur within all of us. I will include the dreamer's response that they sent back to me after receiving their dream interpretations to again demonstrate to you the absolute accuracy (and ease) of using the Dreamtime Method.

I'll see you in Chapter Five!

CHAPTER FIVE

Interpreting Common Dream Themes
Using the Dreamtime Method

In this chapter, I have interpreted common dream themes that we all see and experience in our dreams. I will give you my understanding of why these dream themes so commonly occur within all of us. I have included the dreamer's response that they sent back to me after receiving their dream interpretations to show you the absolute accuracy (and ease) of using the Dreamtime Method to interpret your own dreams.

All of the following dreams in this chapter that I am interpreting are dreams that have been sent to me with approval to be interpreted anonymously.

Common Dream Themes

The Recurring or "Repeat" Dream

I will begin with a common dream theme that I interpret in dreams all of the time. This is the recurring or "repeat" dream theme. A recurring or repeat dream is when you dream the same dream *over and over again* with the same dream symbols. Recurring and repeat dream themes can occur night after night or at different time intervals in our lives, sometimes years apart.

When you have a recurring (repeat) dream, there is one of two issues going on within you and your everyday, three-dimensional life.

↦ You are either "consciously" understanding what your dream communication is telling you and not making the necessary changes accordingly in your everyday life

↦ Or you do not understand what your dream is communicating to you and your DreamSelf is giving you the same dream over and over again until you *get its meaning!*

Recurring and repeat dreams indicate that "karmic" situations are going on within you and your life. Karmic situations are repetitive actions and circumstances that you have previously experienced and are now recreating to experience again. The reason that you may be repeating them is possibly you have not understood the meaning of the experience for you and your life in the past so you are recreating it again to try to understand its meaning now. Also, you may be recreating your experience again to complete it.

Here's an example of a "Recurring" or repeat dream interpreted using the Dreamtime Method.

Dear Dreamtime,

I have a recurring dream that my car has been stolen. I come out of a store or work and look for my car and it is gone! I report it stolen and never get it back. Can you tell me what this dream means?

Dreamer

Dear Dreamer,

(Note to the reader: The following two paragraphs of introduction are what I use when interpreting people's dreams to briefly explain the Dreamtime Method. I will only use this introduction in this initial dream interpretation so as not to be redundant in the subsequent interpreted dreams.)

Your dreams are *energy* from within you that is a communication from your own all-knowing Guidance that lies within. This part of you is your own Divine Self and I will now refer to it as I interpret this dream as your DreamSelf Within. As your DreamSelf Within communicates your dream to you, this part of you, as its method of communication to you, *imagines and thinks* of each of your dream symbols as though each symbol is a created physical aspect and ability that you now possess from within.

Understanding this, as I interpret your dream using the Dreamtime Method, I interpret and explain each of your dream symbols as though each is then an aspect, power, and ability of your own energy that you now possess. Interpreting your dream and dream symbols in this way (the Dreamtime Method) gives you an absolutely accurate interpretation of your dream because this is the way your DreamSelf Within created your dream as it communicated it to you.

Whenever you have a recurring dream, there is one of two issues going on within your life. You are either "consciously" understanding what your dream communication is telling you and not making necesary changes accordingly in your life. Or you might not understand what your dream is communicating to you and therefore your DreamSelf

Within is giving you the same dream theme *over and over* again until you get its meaning!

With this recurring dream, your DreamSelf is communicating to you that within your current thinking and thoughts creating your now . . . your car has been stolen.

Using the Dreamtime Method, I start by taking the everyday definition of a "car." The normal definition of a "car" could be understood as: a vehicle that moves one from "place to place" in their daily living. In this dream, because you say your car has been stolen, your inner DreamSelf is communicating that there is some issue going on in your daily living now (and in the past since this is a recurring dream) where your ability to move from place to place within your own life (your car) is being stolen or robbed from you.

You say that, in your dream, you're always coming out of a store or work, you look around, and your car is just *gone*. A "store" as a dream symbol from your DreamSelf is communicating your "inner store," or your own "inner resources." "Work" as a dream symbol is communicating "the job" within you that now needs to be done, much as your daily work is a job that you do every day.

You either come out of the store (your inner resources) or work (the job that needs to be done now) and your car is gone (your ability to take action on either of these in your life right now). You report the car stolen, but never do get it back. The "action" of reporting the car stolen and then never getting it back is saying that on some level, you consciously know that your ability to move (forward) is being stolen or taken away in your everyday living situation, but you aren't doing anything to help yourself prevent or stop this from happening. This above understanding/interpretation of your dream coupled with the fact that this is a *repeat dream* is saying that your DreamSelf Within is so adamant that you now make some kind of a change in your life that it keeps giving you this same dream over and over again so you will become *consciously aware* of this (karmic) situation in your life and do something about it!

Your dreams not only tell you what's going on in your life, but as your own "multi-dimensional energy" from within attract into your next day and days after dreaming your dream similar three-dimensional (physical energy) to provide the solution for whatever your dream is addressing. It is in this way that your dreams create your everyday, three-dimensional Self and life.

Understanding the above, I would now look for the energy and information to be available of what or who in your everyday living situation is stealing your ability to move forward with your valuable inner resources (your creativity within) and to manifest them in your everyday life. Becoming consciously aware of how you are letting your energy to be taken (stolen) will allow you to then do something about the situation so you can resolve this karmic energy situation and move forward with yourself and your life.

Your multi-dimensional DreamSelf Within that creates your dreams for you is not separate from you! Your DreamSelf Within is the same you that lives within you during waking reality. Your DreamSelf is, however, an unlimited, supernatural dimension of yourself within that *knows and has access* to all things! That means that your DreamSelf knows exactly what you need to do in your life to be whole and fulfilled from within. You can trust its advice!

Please e-mail me back when you get this and let me know if there is anything that you did not understand of how I used the Dreamtime Method to interpret your dream. Thank you again for submitting your dream for interpretation and good dreaming!

Terri Ullstrup
The Dreamtime

Here's the response I received after I sent the above dream interpretation to the Dreamer:

Dear Terri,

As soon as I started reading your dream interpretation of my dream, I knew what it was referring to. This interpretation could not be more "right on" regarding some of the thinking that I have about how I want to make a career change in my life, but end up saying to myself that I could never do it. I realized from how you explained this dream that I have been constantly (over a period of years now) feeding myself negative talk about making any kind of a change.

I'm tired of having this dream over and over and of my negative thinking about myself that I now see from this dream interpretation is actually creating this. Thank you for your insightful interpretation. I'm going to try and change my thinking about this and see if this draining repeat dream goes away for good so I can move ahead with what it is I really want to do.

Dreamer

➻ Reader, as you can see in my interpretation of this "repeat dream," I started with the first dream sentence and interpreted each dream symbol using the Dreamtime Method. I then added those interpretations together in an ordered and logical way so the dreamer could see how I arrived at an understanding of the dream.

➻ With regard to this dreamer, I had no idea what was going on within his or her life when I interpreted this dream using the Dreamtime Method. However, the dream interpretation was absolutely correct and accurate in its interpretation just as yours will be when interpreting your own dreams!

Nightmare Dreams

I often see the common dream theme of a "nightmare." A nightmare dream can be defined as any dream that frightens you. It can involve death and dying, being chased, or anything one considers scary and frightening. Usually with nightmares (a dream that is frightening), you need to be made aware of something that is going on within your life that requires your attention. This is why nightmare dreams are such an effective communication from your DreamSelf Within for creating change. Nightmares get your conscious attention just as soon as you wake up!

Nightmare dreams can also become repeat dreams. Remember that nightmare dreams, just like all of our dreams, are a communication from your inner Self, your DreamSelf Within, that is information (and energy) about what's actively going on within you and your everyday life.

Here's an example of a "Nightmare dream" interpreted using the Dreamtime Method.

Dear Dreamtime,

I had a dream about someone who is trying to rape and kill me. This was a horrible dream and I was terrified. What does this dream mean?

Dreamer

Dear Dreamer,

In this dream, your DreamSelf Within is communicating that within your current thinking and thoughts creating your now . . . you dreamed that someone is trying to rape and kill you.

Using the Dreamtime Method, the commonly understood three-dimensional definition of "rape" is the forceful and violent taking of the "life energy" of another. Your dream symbol of the "act of rape" as a communication from your DreamSelf is saying that right now there is, in some manner, a forceful and violent taking of your own energy that is going on within you and your everyday life.

In your dream, you say that this person is not only trying to rape you, but is also trying to kill you. Murder and the action of killing is defined as the obliteration of someone's life energy as one thinks of in a homicide. Murder in your dream as a dream symbol "action" is communicating from your DreamSelf that because of the extreme energy drain you are experiencing in your daily living situation (from the rape), the situation is coming close to taking your whole life energy away (i.e., the murder).

To pinpoint what this important dream is communicating to you, I would look in your daily living situation for how you may feel that you are constantly being drained against your will of your life energy (the rape) to the point where you feel unable to go on (the murder). I then feel you will have the answer to what this dream is addressing. The depleting of your energy as symbolized by the rape in this dream might be going on within your own thinking and thoughts (you taking your own life energy away by negative thinking) or it may involve someone or something else creating this in your everyday life. Only you will know how these circumstances are occurring within yourself and life.

Your dreams not only *tell* you what's going on in your life, but as your own "multi-dimensional energy" from within attract into your next day and days after dreaming your dream similar three-dimensional (physical energy) to provide the solution for whatever your dream is addressing. It is in this way that your dreams *create* your everyday, three-dimensional reality.

Understanding the above, I would look in the day(s) following this dream for ways to not only be more "aware" of when and where this draining situation is happening, but to then have increased energy available to alter and change whatever it is that is violently taking your vital life energy to the point of destroying it.

Please e-mail me back when you get this and let me know if there is anything that you did not understand of how I used the Dreamtime Method to interpret your dream. Thank you again for submitting your dream for interpretation and good dreaming!

Terri Ullstrup
The Dreamtime

Here is the Dreamer's response to the above Nightmare dream interpretation:

Dear Terri,

Can I say how accurate your interpretation was for what's going on with me in my life? I was amazed! In my work situation, I have a co-worker that is very explosive and tough to be around. This person is an absolute energy drain and it is really now, that I think of it, after reading your right-on dream interpretation, ruining my life! I was really concerned after having this dream that this literally might happen to me, but now with the way you explain and interpret my dream, I'm relieved! I had no idea that dreams could tell you what's going on within your life much less how to deal with life. I'll look for the "energy" to be around to find a new job. Thank you so much!

Dreamer

↳ Reader, with this "nightmare-type dream," you can see how I easily and accurately used the Dreamtime Method to interpret what this extremely important dream communication was saying to the dreamer. Again, I knew nothing of this dreamer's life circumstance as I interpreted his or her dream using the Dreamtime Method. As you interpret *your own dream* using the Dreamtime Method, you should be able to connect your dream interpretation easily and intuitively to what is going on within you and your life!

The Chase Dream

Here's another common theme of the Nightmare Dream, that of being chased.

Dear Dreamtime,

In my dream, a man is chasing me with a knife and I can't run very fast. As he starts to reach me, I wake up. What does this dream mean?

Dreamer

Dear Dreamer,

In this dream, your DreamSelf Within is communicating that within your current thinking and thoughts creating your now . . . you dream that a man is chasing you with a knife.

Within each of us are two types of energy, male and female. Your "male energy" is that part of you within that is your ability *to act* in life and *to take action*. Your male energy as a dream symbol is always represented by the image/figure of a man or men in your dream. Your "female energy" is that other half of you within which is your *intuition*, the doorway to your talents, abilities, and creativity. Your female energy as a dream symbol is always represented by the image/figure of a female or females in your dream.

In this dream, a man is chasing you. The man chasing you as a dream symbol communication from your DreamSelf is saying that there is some action going on within yourself and life (symbolized by the man) that is causing you to feel pursued, hunted, or chased in your everyday living situation.

The man chasing you has a knife. The everyday definition of a knife is a utensil/tool that allows one "to cut" something. Adding this definition/understanding of a knife to the action of the man chasing you is communicating from your DreamSelf that right now, there is some action going on in your daily living (the man) where you are being pursued (chased) to make you aware that you need to cut something (the knife) from you and your life.

In the dream, you go on to say that as the man is chasing you, you don't seem to be able to run very fast. The inability to run very fast to get away from the man with the knife is saying that on some level, you know that taking some action (the man) and cutting out what needs to be eliminated from your life (the knife), that this is really the right thing for you to do. But for some reason in your everyday living situation you are hesitant to do this (you not being able to get away) as there is some fear regarding taking action. The reason that you wake up from the dream as soon as the man starts to reach you is because you intuitively know this is going to be hard to do in your everyday living situation and you don't believe you have the courage to take the action needed.

To get a deeper understanding of what this dream is saying, I would look at what it is in your everyday living situation that is making you feel uneasy (afraid) of moving forward to rid yourself of something that you really do not need in your life. If you can pinpoint that, I feel you will have the answer to what this important dream is addressing.

Your dreams not only *tell* you what's going on in your life, but as your own "multi-dimensional energy" from within attract into your next day and days after dreaming your dream similar three-dimensional (physical energy) to provide the solution for whatever your dream is addressing. It is in this way that your dreams *create* your everyday, three-dimensional reality.

Understanding the above, I would look in your next day(s) after dreaming this dream for the awareness of why you are afraid of making a change and then for the action (energy) to assist yourself to eliminate whatever it is that you don't need that is depleting and harming you and your life energy.

Please e-mail me back when you get this and let me know if there is anything that you did not understand of how I used the Dreamtime Method to interpret your dream. Thank you again for submitting your dream for interpretation and good dreaming!

Terri Ullstrup
The Dreamtime

Here's the Dreamer's response to the above Chase dream interpretation:

Dear Terri,

Thank you for your insightful dream interpretation. I am in an abusive relationship that I know needs to go. I've been dragging my feet about making the break (cut) and the dream interpretation that you did spelled this out to me. I know I have options and need to look at them. I also am going to purchase your dream interpretation book as your easy to understand dream interpretation peeked my interest not only in terms of your method, but in seeing what my future dreams may be guiding me to do. Thank you so much.

Dreamer

Death Dreams

Another common dream theme I see frequently is "death." Death dream themes are very common and usually are not to be taken literally. I will use the Dreamtime Method to interpret the following Death Dream.

Dear Dreamtime,

I dreamed I was in a darkly lit room. Someone told me that my father had died. I woke up feeling very upset and worried. What does this dream mean?

Dreamer

Dear Dreamer,

With this dream, your DreamSelf Within is communicating that within your current thinking and thoughts creating your now . . . you are in a darkly lit room.

Using the Dreamtime Method, the everyday, physical definition of a "house" can be thought of as a physical place where one lives. The everyday physical definition of a "room" can be viewed as a sectioned area within a house. The common everyday definition of a "darkly lit" room would be a room with little or no light. Taking the above under-standings and adding them together, your DreamSelf in this dream is communicating that within you right now (the house) there is a certain portion of you (the room) that has very little awareness and information (the room being darkly lit) of certain issues that are going on within your everyday Self and your life.

In the dream, someone told you that your father had died. Within each of us are two types of energy, male and female. Your "male energy" is that part of you within that is your ability to act in life and *to take action*. Your male energy as a dream symbol is always represented by the image/figure of a man or men in your dream. Your "female energy" is that other half of you within which is your *intuition*, the doorway to your talents, abilities, and creativity. Your female energy as a dream symbol is always represented by the image/figure of a female or females in your dream.

When you dream of other people that you know in waking reality, whatever you feel and associate with them is what you are looking at within yourself. In other words, it is like looking into a mirror. The other people that you are dreaming about in the dream are reflecting back to you the aspects and abilities of what you associate with them that you possess similarly within yourself. In understanding this, it means that the dream information being communicated to you in your dream from your DreamSelf regarding that person is actually about you, not them.

The everyday, generic definition of a "father" is a male parent who takes action to provide guidance, support, and nurturing for his child, much as a father should do in everyday life. You did not tell me what you felt about your father in waking reality so you will have to fill in the blanks there. But in general, putting the above dream symbol understandings together, your father dying in your dream is communicating from your DreamSelf that within your life right now, your own ability to nurture your own inner child (your father), that this has died within you (symbolized by the action of your father dying in your dream).

"Darkness" as in little or low light in a dream always interprets to mean that there is "limited awareness" and not a lot of insight (light) going on within you for whatever issue your dream is addressing. Taking the above interpretation/understandings together, coupled with the room in your dream being darkly lit, your dream interprets to mean that right now, regarding the responsibility and caring of your inner child (your hopes and dreams for your life), you have little or no insight of how you are letting this die within yourself and life. To get a better idea of what this dream is communicating, I would look at where in your life you have failed to listen to your dreams (your inner child) and to nurture and care for them (your father) to the point that it is now totally gone (your father dying).

Your dreams not only *tell* you what's going on in your life, but as your own "multi-dimensional energy" from within attract into your next day and days after dreaming your dream similar three-dimensional (physical energy) to provide the solution for whatever your dream is addressing. It is in this way that your dreams *create* your everyday, three-dimensional reality.

Understanding the above, I would look for ways (the energy) in your next day(s) after dreaming this dream to become more aware of how you are creating the present circumstances of ignoring and not acting on your inner hopes, desires, and undeveloped creativity so that you can move forward and take action for yourself in a positive way!

Please e-mail me back when you get this and let me know if there is anything that you did not understand of how I used the Dreamtime Method to interpret your dream. Thank you again for submitting your dream for interpretation and good dreaming!

Terri Ullstrup
The Dreamtime

Here's the dreamer's response to the above Death Dream interpretation:

Dear Terri,

I read your dream interpretation response with much interest. After dreaming this dream, I called my father who is alive and well, but this dream sure scared me! You hit the nail right on the head with your interpretation. My father never pursued his dreams in life and I am not doing the work I want to do. I have pretty much accepted the fact that I'm not going to be able to do what I really want with my life. I need to do something, because after getting this dream, I realize how deeply this is affecting me.

And guess what! I got a call from a friend who wants me to do some freelancing for him. I guess like you said, the "energy" comes in for you! Thank you for your help and understanding of this scary dream.

Dreamer

➻ Reader, as you can see from the above death dream, most people are very concerned that a death and dying dream is precognitive of what is going to happen in their life. And as you can see from how I interpreted the above death dream and from the dreamer's response, that was not the case! Your dream symbols need to be interpreted as your DreamSelf Within communicates them to you. And that is always multi-dimensionally, and in most instances, not literally.

"Other People You Know" from Waking Reality in Your Dream

Another common dream theme, which was touched upon in the last section, is when you dream of other people who you know in your waking reality. Other people in your dream can be anyone you know or people who you don't personally know, celebrities, politicians, or anyone. When people dream of other people in their dreams, they always want to insist that the dream is about the person(s) they are dreaming about and not themselves. *Just the opposite is true!*

Your DreamSelf Within creates your dreams as though every dream symbol in your dream is an aspect and ability of yourself. So in order to interpret your dream *accurately and multi-dimensionally*, you must do the same. When you dream about someone else in your dream, whatever you feel about the person(s) you are dreaming about interprets to mean that you are now exhibiting those *same characteristics and traits* comparably. This means that whatever you think and associate in waking reality with the person(s) you are dreaming about, they are then representing and symbolizing what you should be understanding you possess *similarly* within yourself.

I will now give you a dream where the dreamer told me what they felt about the other people in their dream. This is a good example of how you should use the Dreamtime Method to interpret and understand "other people" when you see them in your dreams.

Dear Dreamtime,

I dreamed that I was at a girl's house (I am male), someone who I used to know in high school. She was my girlfriend at the time. She was very popular and fun with everybody, but I have not seen her in years. In my dream, my current girlfriend (in reality) showed up at this old girlfriend's house and was extremely jealous. My girlfriend in real life is not the jealous type. Does this mean that my old girlfriend and I will be reunited? Please tell me what this dream means.

Dreamer

Dear Dreamer,

In this dream, your DreamSelf Within is communicating that within your current thinking and thoughts creating your now . . . you are at an old high-school girlfriend's house.

Within each of us are two types of energy, male and female. Your "male energy" is that part of you within that is your ability *to act* in life and to *take action*. Your male energy as a dream symbol is always represented by the image/figure of a man or men in your dream. Your "female energy" is that other half of you within which is your *intuition*, the doorway to your talents, abilities, and creativity. Your female energy as a dream symbol is always represented by the image/figure of a female or females in your dream.

When you dream of other people that you know in waking reality, whatever you feel and associate with them is what you are looking at within yourself. In other words, it is like looking into a mirror. The other people that you are dreaming about in the dream are reflecting back to you the aspects and abilities of what you associate with them that you possess similarly within yourself. In understanding this, it means that the dream information being communicated to you in your dream from your DreamSelf regarding that person is actually about you, not them.

Using the Dreamtime Method, the normal, everyday understanding of a "high school" is a place to learn and be educated. The everyday understanding of a "house" is a physical place where one lives. Now, in your dream you are at an old high-school girlfriend's house. You said that this girlfriend was very popular and fun.

Putting the above definitions and understandings together and then thinking as your DreamSelf does, this dream is communicating that right now you are learning and being educated (high school) regarding your own "female energy" within (as symbolized by your old high-school girlfriend, she being female). The dream is saying that you should be looking at your own female energy within, your inner talents and abilities, just as you used to think of your old girlfriend's. You said that she was creative, fun, and popular. You should be looking now at your own talents and abilities in the same way symbolized by you being at her "house' where the dream symbol of her house is representing you (the dream symbol of a house generically interprets to mean: you or the "Self").

In the dream, your current girlfriend shows up at your old girlfriend's house and is very jealous that you are there. The dream symbol of your current girlfriend is communicating/representing what you presently think and feel about your own inner creativity now. She represents the attitudes that you have about your own "female energy" within (your own talents and abilities) in your waking reality. She is jealous of your high-school girlfriend in the dream. Your current girlfriend as a dream symbol is communicating/saying that within you right now, you want to learn to have more fun and enjoyment and think better of your creativity and self-worth (just like the high school girlfriend), but whatever it is that you are doing now with your talents and abilities (the present girlfriend), this situation is causing a conflict within your everyday living (symbolized by the emotions of jealousy in your dream).

To get a better idea of what your DreamSelf is communicating in this dream, I would look at how you feel conflicted about valuing your talents, abilities, and creativity and having some fun with them versus what you are doing with them now. I feel that then you will have the answer to what this important dream is addressing.

Your dreams not only *tell* you what's going on in your life, but as your own "multi-dimensional energy" from within attract into your next day and days after dreaming your dream similar three-dimensional (physical energy) to provide the solution for whatever your dream is addressing. It is in this way that your dreams *create* your everyday, three-dimensional reality.

Understanding the above, I would look for the way (energy) in your next day(s) after dreaming this dream to help you to reconcile what it is you want to do now with your creativity versus what you are currently doing, so that you may have more fun and pleasure. And dreamer, this issue is very important because it is a *life lesson* you are learning (as symbolized by the dream symbol of "high school"). As to whether you and your old girlfriend will be reunited . . . well, as you can see by how I interpreted this dream, this dream is *about you and your inner creativity*, not whether you and your old girlfriend will get back together!

Please e-mail me back when you get this and let me know if there is anything that you did not understand of how I used the Dreamtime Method to interpret your dream. Thank you again for submitting your dream for interpretation and good dreaming!

Terri Ullstrup
The Dreamtime

Here's the Dreamer's response to the above dream interpretation:

Dear Terri,

You could not have been more accurate with this dream interpretation. I am going through what seems to be a mid-life crisis about my work. I am a highly paid professional, but not having much fun. I find myself daydreaming about doing something totally different, but always get pulled back into the reality that I couldn't possibly do anything else than what I'm doing now (i.e. the conflict in the dream). I had no idea that the dream symbols in my dream could tell me this. I really thought this dream was telling me to look up my old girlfriend, but your interpretation makes perfect sense. I need your dream book to learn your method, quite interesting. Thank you!

Dreamer

Sex Dreams

The next dream theme that is very common and that I always receive questions about is what I call the "sex" dream theme. Sex dreams occur all the time, but people can feel very uncomfortable talking about them or trying to understand what they mean. I will now give you an example of a "sex dream" and how you should interpret this "action/symbol" in your dreams using the Dreamtime Method.

Dear Dreamtime,

I have had a repeat dream of having intercourse with an old boyfriend. I am happily married now to a great guy and am increasingly worried about this. Can you help and tell me what this means?

Dreamer

Dear Dreamer,

Whenever you have a recurring dream, there is one of two issues going on within your life. You are either *consciously* understanding what the dream communication is telling you and not making the necessary changes in your life. Or you do not understand what the dream is communicating to you and your DreamSelf Within is giving you the same dream theme over and over again until you understand what it means.

In this dream, your DreamSelf Within is communicating that within your current thinking and thoughts creating your now . . . you are having intercourse with your old boyfriend.

Within each of us are two types of energy, male and female. Your "male energy" is that part of you within that is your ability *to act* in life and *to take action*. Your male energy as a dream symbol is always represented by the image/figure of a man or men in your dream. Your "female energy" is that other half of you within which is your *intuition*, the doorway to your talents, abilities, and creativity. Your female energy as a dream symbol is always represented by the image/figure of a female or females in your dream.

The three-dimensional definition of sexual intercourse can be defined as the physical merger of a male and a female's energy. Sexual intercourse as a dream symbol of communication from your DreamSelf multi-dimensionally symbolizes the merger within you of your own "male energy" (your inner ability to act and take action in your life) with your own inner "female energy" (your intuition, creativity, talents, and abilities).

In this dream, you were having intercourse with your old boyfriend. When you dream of other people that you know in waking reality, whatever you feel and associate with them is what you are looking at within yourself. In other words, it is like looking into a mirror. The other people that you are dreaming about in the dream are reflecting back to you the aspects and abilities of what you associate with them that you possess similarly within yourself. In understanding this, it means that the dream information being communicated to you in your dream from your DreamSelf regarding them is actually about you, not them.

From the above definitions of male and female energy and what it means when you dream of other people who you know in waking reality, your old boyfriend is symbolizing your own *previously created* male energy within or how you "took action" in your life in the past. You did not tell me what you felt and associated with your old boyfriend. If what you felt about him when you dated him was positive or if he was a man of action who took definitive direction in and with his life, then your DreamSelf is saying you need now to take similar action in your life to merge (the act of intercourse with your boyfriend) your many talents and abilities (your female energy within) to create a new "you."

If your old boyfriend was indecisive and not an action man, then your inner guidance, your DreamSelf, is saying that right now you are being indecisive and not taking any action to use your creativity in your life as symbolized by you having intercourse (merging energies) with your old boyfriend (his/your old indecisive ways). Since only you know what your old boyfriend was like in the past, you will have to fill in the blanks of what type of action you are now similarly taking in your everyday life.

Your dreams not only *tell* you what's going on in your life, but as your own "multi-dimensional energy" from within attracts into your next day and days after dreaming your dream similar three-dimensional (physical energy) to provide the solution for whatever your dream is addressing. It is in this way that your dreams create your everyday, three-dimensional Self and your life.

In understanding the above, I would look in your next day(s) after dreaming this dream for circumstances (the energy) to become available for you to take some "new action" regarding the use of your inner talents, abilities, and creativity to create a totally new direction for you and your life.

Please e-mail me back when you get this and let me know if there is anything that you did not understand of how I used the Dreamtime Method to interpret your dream. Thank you again for submitting your dream for interpretation and good dreaming!

Terri Ullstrup
The Dreamtime

Here's the Dreamer's response to the above Sex Dream interpretation:

Dear Terri,

What relief I had in reading your interpretation as I thought there was some unresolved issue going on with my old boyfriend! I do need to take some action in a decisive way with some creative work I have been thinking about doing for years. My old boyfriend was a "doer" in life, so your dream interpretation makes perfect sense when I think of it in that light. This interpretation has really given me something to think about in moving ahead. Thank you so much!

Dreamer

↦ Reader, as you can see from interpreting the above "sex" dream, I started with the normal definition of "male" and "female" energy. I then coupled the understanding of male energy (the ability to act) with the dreamer's female energy (her creativity, talents, and abilities) to get an absolutely accurate interpretation of this dreamer's sex dream (i.e., the sexual intercourse happening in the dream). I obtained this accurate dream interpretation by thinking *multi-dimensionally* or that the dreamer was the central creator in her dream and that all the dream symbols in the dream where aspects and abilities of herself. The interpretation was absolutely correct as evidenced from the dreamer responding that she now needs to take some decisive action on her creativity. When you interpret your sex dreams using the Dreamtime Method, you should interpret these dreams multi-dimensionally and in the same way.

Additionally, using the Dreamtime Method and thinking multi-dimensionally as I did to interpret the above sex dream would also be the way you should understand and interpret your dream (whether you are a male or a female dreaming) when you dream of a man (symbolizing your male energy within) having sexual relations with another male (symbolizing the merger of "additional" male energy within).

Whether you are a male or a female dreaming:

✓ In the instance of dreaming of a male having sexual relations with another male, the correct multi-dimensional interpretation would be that the person dreaming the dream is merging his or her male energy within (his or her ability to act in life) with added "male energy" (the sex with another male) to create increased accelerated movement and action within his or her life. Possibly the dreamer was unmotivated and really needed to take some "definitive action" in their life and that is why their DreamSelf Within created and communicated this type of sex dream.

The same would hold true (whether you are a male or a female dreaming) if you dream of a female (symbolizing your female energy within) having sexual relations with another female (symbolizing the merger of additional female energy within).

✓ In the example of dreaming of a female having sexual relations with another female, the correct multi-dimensional interpretation would be that the person dreaming the dream is merging his or her female energy within (creativity, talents, abilities, and intuition) with added "female energy" (the sex with another female) to produce enhanced and heightened creativity within his or her three-dimensional Self and life. Possibly the dreamer had rare talents and abilities within, but because of low self-esteem and confidence lacked the understanding of this and their DreamSelf created and communicated this type of sex dream so that he or she could become more aware of this energy and manifest accordingly in his or her life.

Cleansing Dreams

Another dream theme I see frequently in dreams is the "cleansing" dream. Cleansing dreams are experienced in your dreams as dream themes of *release, rebirth, purification, cleansing, and elimination.*

➻ The dream symbols frequently seen in cleansing dreams are bathroom symbols such as toilets, bathtubs, showers, etc. They can also involve laundering your clothes, cleaning your house, washing your hair, or any similar dream symbols and action.

The timing of when you will experience cleansing dreams can be any time, but this is most frequently seen when the moon is full. The action of the moon's energy, as described in Chapter Two, is always that of cleansing, purification, and elimination for you and your life. When the moon is full, you are getting the full "light" of the 10th dimensional consciousness of your DreamSelf being reflected and communicated to you in your dream. This understanding compares your dream energy dreamed during a full moon to that of a flashlight. Your DreamSelf Within is shining your inner flashlight on you to make you aware of situations and issues within your Self and your life that need to be cleansed, purified, and/or eliminated for you to move forward.

Here's an example of a "cleansing" dream:

Dear Dreamtime,

I am female and my dream involves an immediate need to use a public bathroom. However, the women's bathroom is filthy with disgusting overflowing toilets in every single stall and no toilet paper. Please explain what this disturbing dream means.

Dreamer

Dear Dreamer,

With this dream, your DreamSelf Within is communicating that within your current thinking and thoughts creating your now . . . there is an immediate need for you to use a public bathroom.

The normal, everyday definition of a "public" bathroom is a place available to all for elimination and cleansing. A public bathroom as a dream symbol from your DreamSelf is communicating and referring to your ability within to create a complete over-all cleansing and elimination for all of your Self and life.

In your dream, there is an immediate need to use this facility. This action as a communication from your DreamSelf is saying that right now, in your everyday living, there is an urgent and immediate need for an all encompassing elimination and cleansing (the public bathroom) of yourself and your life. In the public bathroom, the toilets are filthy, overflowing, and there is no toilet paper available in any stall. Using the Dreamtime Method, the everyday physical definition of a toilet is a "seat/position" for defecation, urination, and general physical elimination. The everyday understanding of toilet paper could be thought of as being an "aid" to cleaning up after using a toilet.

Putting the above definitions/understandings together, multiple, dirty over-flowing toilets with no available toilet paper as a dream symbol communication from your

DreamSelf is saying that within you right now, there is an over-all *inability* to eliminate negative emotions (urination) and repugnant thinking about yourself (defecation) that has brought you to a point where you are plugged, stopped up, and in immediate need of release (the dirty over-flowing toilets). I feel the dream information of no toilet paper being available is communicating that in your everyday life right now, you are also not making any efforts to assist yourself (the toilet paper) in getting rid of (eliminating) these negative thoughts and emotions. Because you said that in the dream every single one of the bathroom stalls were stopped up and overflowing, I believe this unfortunate situation is occurring within all areas your life right now, within your body, your mind, and your spirit.

You said that in "waking reality," you are female and that in your dream it was you (as a female) in the public restroom. Within each of us are two types of energy, male and female. Your "male energy" is that part of you within that is your ability *to act* in life and *to take action*. Your male energy as a dream symbol is always represented by the image/figure of a man or men in your dream. Your "female energy" is that other half of you within which is your *intuition*, the doorway to your talents, abilities, and creativity. Your female energy as a dream symbol is always represented by the image/figure of a female or females in your dream.

Keeping the above definition of "female energy" in mind, since you are female in waking reality and you *are* the female in your dream looking at this unkempt public restroom, I believe your dream is communicating that the energy that needs to be cleansed and eliminated has to do with negative emotions and thinking you may have going on regarding your own inner creativity and self-worth (your female energy within). To further pinpoint what this important dream is communicating, I would look at how and where in your daily living situation you (and/or possibly others) are constantly saying and thinking negatives about you (in every avenue of your life) and I feel you will then have the answer to this dream.

Your dreams not only tell you what's going on in your life, but as your own "multi-dimensional energy" from within attracts into your next day and days after dreaming your dream similar three-dimensional (physical energy) to provide the solution for whatever your dream is addressing. It is in this way that your dreams create your everyday, three-dimensional Self and your life.

In understanding the above, you should look in your next day(s) after dreaming this dream for increased awareness (the energy) of how you are being receptive and/or contributing to negative "self-talk" and thinking regarding your inner talents, abilities, and self-worth. And of how this behavior is causing you to have emotional overload. This awareness and knowing can then assist you to change and eliminate this unneeded thinking and improve (cleanse) your life on a daily basis.

Please e-mail me back when you get this and let me know if there is anything that you did not understand of how I used the Dreamtime Method to interpret your dream.

Thank you again for submitting your dream for interpretation and good dreaming!

Terri Ullstrup
The Dreamtime

Here's the Dreamer's response to the above Cleansing dream interpretation:

Dear Terri,

Thank you for interpreting my dream. I was embarrassed leaving such a disgusting dream! Your dream interpretation was exact in that I pretty much always do think and talk poorly of myself and then dwell on those thoughts. I grew up in an abusive family who talked and acted this way all the time. I realize from how you interpreted my dream that I need to let go and get rid of this negative thinking about myself. Now that I am more aware of this from your dream interpretation, I realize that I allow others in my life put me down too. I need to make some changes. Thank you again for my "DreamSelf's guidance."

Dreamer

Animal and Insect Dreams

The next common dream theme that I see frequently in dreams involve the dreamer dreaming about animals, insects, or non-human creatures. I will now use the Dreamtime Method to interpret the following non-human creature dream.

Dear Dreamtime,

I had a dream where there were snakes and spiders that were trying to get me. Some were poisonous and others weren't. I'm terrified of both of these! Can you help me and tell me what this dream means?

Dreamer

Dear Dreamer,

With this dream, your DreamSelf Within is communicating that within your current thinking and thoughts creating your now . . . snakes and spiders are trying to get you.

Using the Dreamtime Method, the three-dimensional definition and understanding of a snake is a creature (reptile, serpent) that has no legs yet has the ability to "move" with much power in life. The three-dimensional definition of a spider is a creature (an insect) that has many legs and the ability within to create a "web."

Thinking as your DreamSelf does, the dream symbols of multiple snakes and spiders is communicating from your DreamSelf that within you right now, you have powerful energies moving (within you and your life) as symbolized by the snakes. Along with these powerful energies (the snakes), you also possess an "inner ability" to create and manifest with these powers (as in how spiders can create and spin a "web"). The snakes and spiders trying to "get you" in your dream are your own powerful creative energies within (the snakes and spiders) trying to get your "attention" so that you will manifest and make them happen in your daily life.

In the dream, you said that some of the snakes and spiders were poisonous and others were not. The non-poisonous snakes and spiders as dream symbols are communicating from your DreamSelf your innate ability to move with power and be creative in your everyday life. Some of the snakes and spiders *being* poisonous is communicating to you that there is some issue (going on within) where you feel that if you use your "power," it could possibly lead to situations that may turn out to be poisonous or toxic to you, your life, and/or others. You said that in waking reality, you are terrified of both snakes and spiders. Since waking reality mirrors the dream state, this is communicating that there are issues going on within yourself where you fear your own power (of creation) as though it may be too much power and/or that you may misuse it.

To get a better understanding of what this important dream is communicating, I would look at what it is that you have been thinking about "creating" or doing with your life right now. Think of how you would feel if you acted on that. I would also consider what you (and/or others) have made you believe would happen that may be negative if you moved forward with your creative energy.

Your dreams not only tell you what's going on in your life, but as your own "multidimensional energy" attract into you the next day(s) after dreaming your dream, similar threedimensional (physical energy) to provide the solution for whatever your dream is addressing. It is in this way that your dreams create your everyday, three-dimensional Self and life.

In understanding the above, I would look for opportunities and the circumstances (energy) to come into your life in your next day(s) after dreaming this dream to act on what it is you want to create in your life right now. As you take this creative action, try to be aware of the outcome seeing if it helps or hinders you and your life. Then you can make a conscious decision to continue with it or not.

Please e-mail me back when you get this and let me know if there is anything that you did not understand of how I used the Dreamtime Method to interpret your dream. Thank you again for submitting your dream for interpretation and good dreaming!

Terri Ullstrup
The Dreamtime

Here's the Dreamer's response to the above Animal/Insect Dream interpretation:

Dear Terri,

I was astounded at your very accurate interpretation! I could not for the life of me understand what this dream meant with the snakes and spiders that I so dislike. Your interpretation was spot on in that I have always been afraid to do much of anything new. I come from a very strict religious upbringing where new information and thinking is not embraced. I always think about making changes in my life, but worry that they won't work out or what others may think or that they might disapprove. Your interpretation has given me much to think about. Many thanks.

Dreamer

In Review

As you can see from the above common dream theme examples that I have interpreted using the Dreamtime Method, it matters not what your dream and dream symbols are to be interpreted! The Dreamtime Method will always accurately interpret your dream and dream symbols multi-dimensionally and easily no matter what they may be! Readers, from these inspiring true dream intrepretations, you can now grasp just how exciting and useful dream intrepretation is as it becomes an active part of your life!

For your review, the Dreamtime Method to interpret your own dreams and dream symbols is as follows:

✓ Write your dream out in your Dream Journal in the exact sequence of events that occurred in your dream. Then take each dream symbol in your dream sentence in the order that they occurred using the Dreamtime Method to interpret each one. The Dreamtime Method to interpret your dream symbols is as follows:

- You start by taking the normal three-dimensional definition and understanding for the dream symbol.

- You then think of that understanding as your DreamSelf Within does, which is that you *are* the actual physical, three-dimensional definition/energy of your dream symbol. By "thinking" in this way, you interpret your dream symbol's definition and understanding as your DreamSelf Within does, which is as though your dream symbol's meaning is now a "physical aspect, power, and ability" that you now three-dimensionally have and possess from within.

- As you *think in this way*, the information you receive gives you an absolutely accurate interpretation of your dream symbol.

✓ Lastly, add all of your Dreamtime Dream interpretations together sentence by sentence in the order they occurred in your dream which will give you the complete thoughts of communication of what your DreamSelf is saying to you. This then gives you an absolutely "accurate" multi-dimensional interpretation of your whole dream.

What's Ahead

As you interpret your dreams, you will see numbers and alphabet letters as dream symbols. In Chapter Six, I will teach you how to easily (and multi-dimensionally) interpret numbers and alphabet letters using the Dreamtime Method. You also received a Dreamtime Dreamwheel with your *Dreamtime Dream Interpretation* book. I'll show you how to use your Dreamtime Dreamwheel, which is a fun tool to use as you learn the Dreamtime Method to accurately interpret your dreams.

In closing, people always say that they don't remember their dreams and they ask me how they can do this, so I'll also go over successful techniques for remembering dreams. Want to "program" your dream for your heart's desire? You'll find out how in the next chapter.

See you in Chapter Six!

CHAPTER SIX

Dreamtime Extras!

Interpreting Numbers & Alphabet Letters
Techniques for Remembering & Programming Your Dreams
How to Use the Dreamtime Dreamwheel

In Chapter Six, Dreamtime Extras, I will start by using the Dreamtime Method to demonstrate to you how to interpret numbers and alphabet "letters" commonly seen in your dreams as dream symbols.

Interpreting Numbers in Your Dreams

Your dream symbols of *numbers* are also "dream energy" and have as much *vibratory power* and significance as any of your everyday dream symbols you dream in your dreams. Pay attention to them and interpret them as an important dream communication from your DreamSelf Within!

We'll start with the number "1."

Using the Dreamtime Method for interpreting the number "1," I start with the three-dimensional dictionary definition of the number one where the number 1 means an "individual."

Thinking of this definition/meaning as my DreamSelf Within thinks of it, the dream symbol of the number 1 is now a "physical aspect and ability" of my own three-dimensional energy that comes from within. As I think of myself as the numeral 1 and imagine myself now being an individual, the interpretation from "thinking" as my DreamSelf Within does is that my DreamSelf wants to communicate information to me regarding "me" or my individual Self and life.

The dream symbol of the number 1 refers to and should then be interpreted to mean "You, your individual Self and life."

1 = You, your individual Self and life

Let's move on to number "2."

Quite simply, the three-dimensional dictionary definition of the number "2" is one more than one.

Thinking as my DreamSelf Within *thinks*, the number 2 is now a "physical aspect and ability" of my own three-dimensional energy that comes from within. As I think of myself as the numeral 2 and imagine myself now being "one" more than one, the interpretation I get from "thinking" as my DreamSelf Within does is that my DreamSelf wants to communicate information to me regarding myself (1) plus "another me" (1) or the "balance" of myself within, which is the number 2.

Using the Dreamtime Method, the dream symbol of the number 2 then interprets to mean "balance" or the perfect balance of myself within. This says that the number 2 as a dream symbol should always be interpreted to mean "balance" or the balance of myself within.

2 = balance or the balance of yourself within

Now let's look at the number "3."

The three-dimensional dictionary definition of the number "3" is one more than two.

Consistent with the thinking of my DreamSelf Within, the dream symbol of the number 3 is now a "physical aspect and ability" of my own three-dimensional energy that comes from within. As I think of myself as the numeral 3 and imagine myself now being "one" more than two, the interpretation from thinking as my DreamSelf Within does is that my DreamSelf is communicating: myself (1) plus the balance of myself within (2) which equals the number 3.

As a dream symbol communication from my DreamSelf, the number 3 means the Triangle of myself within or my physical body, my mind, and my Spirit. Three as a dream communication from my DreamSelf is interpreted as my physical body, my mind, and my Spirit.

Any "triangle" dream symbol dreamed in a dream should be interpreted as referring to your body, your mind, and your Spirit. The number 3 should always be interpreted as referring to (the Triangle of) your physical body, your mind, and your Spirit within.

3 = (The Triangle of) your physical body, your mind, and your Spirit within

Next up is the number "4."

The three-dimensional dictionary definition of the number "4" is one more than three.

Following how my DreamSelf Within *thinks*, the dream symbol of the number 4 is now a "physical aspect and ability" of my own three-dimensional energy that comes from within. As I think of myself as the numeral 4 and imagine myself now being "one" more than three, the interpretation I get from thinking as my DreamSelf Within does is that the number 4 is communicating: the Triangle of the myself within (3) plus another me (1) which equals the number 4.

As a dream symbol communication from my DreamSelf, the number 4 means the triangle of myself within (my body, mind, and Spirit) plus another myself (1) which creates a "square" or the "four points or corners" of myself within. The numeral four as a dream communication from my DreamSelf represents my inner square or the foundation of myself and life within.

Any "square" seen as a dream symbol in a dream should be interpreted as referring to your "inner foundation" or the foundation of yourself within. The number 4 always means and should be interpreted as a "foundation" number and is referring to the foundation of yourself and your life within.

4 = a foundation number, the foundation of yourself and your life within

Our next number is "5."

The three-dimensional dictionary definition of the number "5" is one more than four.

Thinking as my DreamSelf Within does, I now take the number 5 to be a "physical aspect and ability" of my own three-dimensional energy that comes from within. As I think of myself as the numeral 5 and imagine myself now being "one" more than four, the interpretation I get is that my DreamSelf is communicating: the foundation of myself within (4) plus another me (1) which equals the number 5.

As a dream symbol communication from my DreamSelf, the number 5 means another myself (1) added to the foundation of the Self (4) which creates "change within." The numeral five as a dream communication from my DreamSelf interprets to mean "a change" or a change going on within the foundation of myself and life within.

Any "pentagram" dreamed as a dream symbol in your dream refers to a change going on within yourself and your life. The number 5 is always interpreted and is referring to a change going on within you and your life.

5 = a change going on within you and your life

Let's look at the number "6."

The three-dimensional dictionary definition of the number "6" is one more than five.

Thinking as my DreamSelf Within does, I now think of the number 6 to be a "physical aspect and ability" of my own three-dimensional energy that comes from within. As I think of myself as the numeral 6 and imagine myself now being "one" more than five, the communication from my DreamSelf is a change going on within myself (5) plus another me (1) which equals the number 6. The number six can also be understood as the Triangle of myself within (3) doubled (3 + 3 = 6).

As a dream symbol communication from my DreamSelf, the number 6 means the triangle of myself within above (which is referring to my non-physical, multi-dimensional DreamSelf Within) added to the triangle of myself below (which is my physical, three-dimensional Self and life). This creates and equals the number 6, which symbolizes my DreamSelf Within which is my "inner guidance." The numeral 6 as a dream communication from my DreamSelf means: inner guidance (which is my DreamSelf Within).

Any "hexagram" dreamed as a dream symbol in a dream refers to and interprets to mean your DreamSelf Within, which is your "inner guidance." The number 6 is always interpreted as a "guidance" number and is referring to your DreamSelf Within.

6 = a guidance number, your DreamSelf Within

Now let's turn our attention to the number "7."

The three-dimensional dictionary definition of the number 7 is one more than six.

Thinking of this definition/meaning as my DreamSelf Within thinks of it, the dream symbol of the number 7 is now a "physical aspect and ability" of my own three-dimensional energy that comes from within. As I think of myself as the numeral 7 and imagine myself now being "one" more than six, my DreamSelf Within is communicating: my inner guidance (6) plus another me (1) which equals the number 7.

As a dream symbol communication from my DreamSelf, the number 7 interprets to mean my inner guidance, my DreamSelf Within (6), plus another Self (1) added which creates the number 7 or a "new cycle of vibration" of myself within.

The numeral 7 as a dream communication from your DreamSelf should be interpreted as a new cycle of vibration within yourself and your life. The number 7 always interprets to mean and is referring to a "new cycle" going on within you and your life.

7 = a new cycle of vibrational energy going on within you and your life

Next is the number "8."

The three-dimensional, dictionary definition of the number "8" is one more than seven.

Thinking as my DreamSelf Within thinks, I take the dream symbol of the number 8 to now be a "physical aspect and ability" of my own three-dimensional energy that comes from within. As I think of myself as the numeral 8 and imagine myself now being "one" more than seven, the interpretation from my DreamSelf that I get is that the number 8 is communicating: a new cycle within me (7) plus another me added (1) which equals the number 8. The number 8 can also be understood as the "foundation" of myself within doubled (4 + 4 = 8).

As a dream symbol communication from my DreamSelf, the number 8 then means the foundation (the number 4) of myself within above (which is my multi-dimensional DreamSelf's non-physical foundation) added to the physical foundation of myself and my life (the number 4) which then creates the "manifestation" of my multi-dimensional energy on the physical plane. Thinking in this way, the numeral 8 as a dream communication from my DreamSelf is interpreted as my ability within to "manifest" on the physical plane and in the material world.

The numeral 8 always interprets to mean and is referring to your ability to "manifest" in the physical world, the material plane.

8 = your ability to manifest in the physical world, the material plane

Now we'll look at the number "9."

The three-dimensional dictionary definition of the number "9" is one more than eight.

In accordance with how my DreamSelf Within thinks, the dream symbol of the number 9 is now a "physical aspect and ability" of my own three-dimensional energy that comes from within. As I think of myself as the numeral 9 and imagine myself now being "one" more than eight, my DreamSelf Within is communicating: my ability within to manifest (8) plus another me (1) which equals the number 9.

As a dream symbol communication from my DreamSelf, the number 9 means another me (1) added to my ability to manifest and create physically (8) which equals the number 9, or the "completion" of myself within. The numeral 9 as a dream symbol communication from my DreamSelf then interprets to mean a "completion number" or the completion of myself within.

The numeral 9 should always be interpreted to mean and is referring to a "completion" going on within you and your life.

9 = a completion going on within you and your life

Last we have the number "10."

The three-dimensional dictionary definition of the number "10" is one more than nine.

Thinking as my DreamSelf Within *thinks*, I imagine the dream symbol of the number 10 as a "physical aspect and ability" of my own three-dimensional energy that comes from within. As I think of myself as the numeral 10 and imagine myself now being "one" more than nine, the interpretation I get from thinking as my DreamSelf Within does is that my DreamSelf is communicating: the number 1 (myself) plus 9 which equals the number 10.

As a dream symbol communication from my DreamSelf, the number 10 means myself (1) added to the power of zero (0) which creates added energy to myself and a higher, faster "vibration" of myself within (the number 10). This means that the numeral 10 as a dream symbol communication from my DreamSelf refers to and should be interpreted as a higher "octave" of vibrational energy within myself and my life.

The numeral "10" should always be interpreted to mean and is referring to a higher "octave" of vibrational energy going on within you and your life.

10 = a higher octave of vibrational energy going on within you and your life

In summary, using the Dreamtime Method to interpret the basic numbers of 1 to 10, their interpreted dream meanings are as follows:

1 = yourself
2 = the balance of yourself within
3 = the triangle of yourself within, your body, your mind and your Spirit
4 = the foundation of yourself and your life within
5 = a change going on within yourself and your life
6 = your inner Guidance, which is your DreamSelf Within
7 = a new cycle of vibrational energy going on within yourself and your life
8 = your ability to manifest and create in the physical, material world
9 = a completion going on within yourself and your life
10 = a higher octave of vibrational energy going on within you and your life

When Numbers Are Combined

Anytime that zeros are added to the basic numbers, it increases *the power* of the original numerical interpretations given above. For example, if you had a dream with the number 5,000, the dream symbol number 5,000 would interpret to mean: change (5) is coming into your life right now in a big way (the 3 zeros added to 5). The number 90,000 would indicate: a completion (9) in a very large and expansive way that is now taking place within you and your everyday life (the 4 zeros added to 9).

With numerals other than zeros added such as the number 1 added to the number 7 as in the number 17 for example, you reduce the sum of numbers to a single digit (1 + 7 = 8). However, keep the "individual" number interpretation/meanings in mind. In our example of the number 17, consider the meaning of the individual number "1" (the Self or you) along with the meaning of the number "7" (a new cycle going on within you). But ultimately with the number 17, you should add the numbers together to get a single digit (1+ 7) or the number 8. The number 8 as a dream symbol interprets to mean that right now you (the number 1) are in a new cycle (the number 7) of material manifestation within your Self and life (the number 8).

Interpreting "Alphabet Letters" Seen in Your Dreams
Using the Dreamtime Method

Oftentimes you will experience "alphabet letters" in your dreams. Using the Dreamtime Method, alphabet letters seen in your dreams should be corresponded to the basic 1 through 9 numbers above with their meanings used accordingly as interpretations.

Interpreting "Alphabet Letters" through numbers:

1	2	3	4	5	6	7	8	9
A	B	C	D	E	F	G	H	I
J	K	L	M	N	O	P	Q	R
S	T	U	V	W	X	Y	Z	

For example, if you dreamed of the alphabet letters B and G, with the alphabet letter B (which matches with the number 2) and G (which matches with the number 7), you would add the numbers corresponding to those letters together: (2 + 7 = 9). You then would take the number 9 and its interpreted meaning of "a completion" that is now going on within you and your life, as the dream interpretation meaning of your dreamed alphabet letters B and G.

If you dreamed of alphabet letters that added to a double digit as for example, the number 15, you would then reduce the number 15 to a single digit or the number 6 (1 + 5 = 6). You would interpret the number 15's meaning as defined above for the number 6: your inner guidance, which is your DreamSelf Within.

If there are "names" in your dream, for an accurate understanding of what the name interprets to mean, correspond the numbers to the alphabet letters in the name and add them together to create a single digit number. For example, the name "Ted" corresponds as follows. The letter "T" equals the number 2, the letter "e" equals the number 5, and the letter "d" equals the number 4. Add those numbers together, 2 + 5 + 4 = 11, where the number 11 reduced to a single digit is the number 2. The name Ted numerically then corresponds to the number 2 and should be interpreted to mean a "balance" number.

Dream Techniques for Remembering Your Dreams

When I tell people that I interpret dreams, inevitably someone will say to me, "I don't remember my dreams. What can I do to remember them?" In this section, I am going to share the *tried and true* methods I have discovered for remembering dreams. I have tested these methods on myself and others throughout the years . . . and they work!

When you are not remembering your dreams at all, or just remembering dream fragments, you usually are not bringing your dreams through to your three-dimensional Self consciously. Here is an exercise that will assist you in recalling and remembering your dreams:

✓ Either sit on your bed before you go to sleep or once you are in bed and say to yourself: "Tonight I will have a great dream that I will remember, understand, and write down, whose advice I will follow, as it easily and effortlessly *creates* my tomorrow."

✓ Say this out loud to yourself three times. Saying this out loud to yourself grounds your non-physical dream energy mentally and physically putting into motion the process of communicating to your DreamSelf that you want to remember your dream.

I know this sounds simple, but this exercise works and will allow you to realize that it is easy to have a *conscious* two-way communication between you and your multi-dimensional DreamSelf! Tell your DreamSelf what you want to do and it will be happy you are making contact. Your DreamSelf will respond and do what you have asked it to do! If you do this exercise to remember your dreams, you will find that it works, the reason being is that you *are* your DreamSelf Within and in command! To increase the future possibility that you will remember your dreams, after doing this exercise and receiving your dream from your DreamSelf, *make sure you write your dream down!*

Another technique to use, if you don't have a dream you remember, is to say to yourself after waking up the next morning, "Today, I will have a trigger in my day that will help me recall my dream of last night." A *"trigger"* can be any three-dimensional energy in your physical day that will connect you in that day to the dream energy of the previous night that you have not remembered.

An example of this may be that when you wake up in the morning, your dream energy seems very close as you were just dreaming. However you can't remember anything. What to do? Ask your *waking* physical Self for a "trigger symbol" of your dream as your day goes on.

How this would then play out in your day may be that you have gone to work, are in your office . . . you look out the window and see a red car driving down the street. Suddenly after seeing the red car drive by, you *recall* that in your dream last night *you were riding in a red car!* The red car is the trigger *symbol* that reminded you of the dream you had last night. But how and why does this happen?

The reason people get *dream symbol triggers* in their three-dimensional days after dreaming that remind them of a specific dream is because their dream symbols *are creating* the energy of their following day(s), as we discussed in previous chapters. Your dream symbols as energy *create* by drawing in similar and like energy, which translates to the energy that is your next three-dimensional day. Understanding the above, this means that trigger symbols *work,* so give this a try!

Programming Your Dreams

As I've discussed, your multi-dimensional dreams are creating your everyday physical three-dimensional Self and life. You can "program a dream" to get information because as you are finding out by now, your dreams *are* your inner guidance which is your ultimate problem-solver!

Whenever you have a problem that you don't know how to solve or what to do, you can program a dream for the solution and get an answer. To do this, sit at your bedside or lie in bed before going to sleep and tell yourself that regarding whatever it is you want answers and solutions for:

» Tonight I will have a great dream regarding (the problem) that I will remember, understand, and write down, whose advice I will then follow, as it easily and effortlessly creates my tomorrow.

» Say this to yourself out loud for three nights before you go to sleep and you will get *your dream answer* which you can then interpret using the Dreamtime Method. Remember, using the Dreamtime Method will give you an absolutely accurate interpretation regarding your dream answer.

You can program your dreams for anything and everything. Prosperity, vital health, great relationships, whatever your heart desires! Remember, when programming a dream, you are talking to the *multi-dimensional you*, the part of yourself within that is infinitely all-knowing, unlimited, and creating your everyday physical Self and life!

Using Your Dreamtime Dreamwheel

With this book, you received an added bonus, the Dreamtime Dreamwheel! Your Dreamtime Dreamwheel is a fun and easy-to-use Quick Reference Guide that is loaded on both sides with dream symbols and their meanings interpreted by using the Dreamtime Method.

On the Dreamtime Dreamwheel, I have interpreted many common dream symbols using the Dreamtime Method. What follows now are the basic instructions of how to use this wheel, but after you have read this book I'm sure you already know now how to interpret your dream symbols using the Dreamtime Method! In saying this, the easy-to-use Dreamtime Dreamwheel can be used to *confirm* your own dream symbol interpretations as you learn and use the Dreamtime Method to interpret your dreams.

On either side of the Dreamwheel are basic and common dream symbols that we all see and experience in our dreams. The instructions on the back of the Dreamwheel state that the first step is to write your dream down (in your Dream Journal) in the proper sequence that your dream occurred.

Next, start with the first dream symbol in the first dream sentence of your dream. Look on the Dreamwheel for your first dream symbol and match it with its corresponding meaning/interpretation. Then write that understanding/meaning down in parenthesis next to your specific dream symbol.

You then continue on with your dream sentence by matching each dream symbol in the order it occurred in your dream sentence with the dream symbol meaning found on the Dreamwheel. When you have finished corresponding your dream symbols in the first sentence of your dream with the meaning/interpretation from the Dreamwheel, then add all of the meanings/interpretations together in the order that they occurred in your dream sentence.

If there are more dream sentences in your dream, interpret each sentence of your dream the same way. After you have interpreted all of your dream sentences, add all the sentence/interpretations together in the order they occurred in your dream to get the *complete thoughts* of what your DreamSelf Within is communicating to you. This gives you an absolutely accurate interpretation of your dream and is *how* your Dreamtime Dreamwheel works!

As discussed, the instructions for using the Dreamtime Dreamwheel are exactly how you would interpret your dream and dreams symbols using the Dreamtime Method. Keep your Dreamtime Dreamwheel in your night stand, backpack, purse . . . whenever or wherever you need a quick dream reference! It's a great Dreamtime resource to have!

What's Ahead

In Chapter Seven, our last chapter, I will complete your *Dreamtime Dream Interpretation* training with the *Triangle for Transforming, your Magician's Wand Within!* You won't want to miss learning about the Triangle for Transforming, the powerful, multi-dimensional technique that accompanies mastering the Dreamtime Method of interpreting your dreams. You've earned it!

I'll see you in Chapter Seven!

CHAPTER SEVEN

Your DreamSelf Is the North Star Within . . .
True, Unchanging, a "Guide"
Your Dreamtime Wrap-Up and Graduation

In this book, you have learned the Dreamtime Method, which is to think as your DreamSelf Within does to multi-dimensionally and accurately interpret your dreams.

You have specifically learned that to think as your DreamSelf Within does, you must imagine that *you are the central creator* of your dreamed dream. That to accurately interpret each of your dream symbols, you must think of each one of them as though you created them. This understanding means that you must think of each of your dream symbols as a created physical aspect and ability of your own Self within.

As I explained in earlier chapters, as you use your DreamsSelf's way *of thinking* to interpret your dreams and consciously connect the information and guidance of them to your everyday Self and life, you raise your physical vibration in the third dimension to that of your 10th dimensional DreamSelf Within. This in turn brings to your everyday waking consciousness the mind-expanding awareness that if you are the creator of your 10th dimensional dream energy, you are also the creator of your three-dimensional physical Self and life. That all you see and experience in your dreams and subsequent physical world are really created aspects *of you* coming from the multi-dimensional power of you.

Accepting Your Whole Multi-Dimensional Self Within

Accepting the above, when you have fascinating, desirable, positive dreams and fun fulfilling experiences in your waking everyday three-dimensional life, it is easy to imagine this energy as being something that you have drawn to you by consciously creating it. But what happens when you have a dream and/or situations occurring in your everyday life that either you don't like or that you could never imagine that you would create?

As I learned to interpret my dreams and realized the *multi-dimensional truth* that

113

my dreams and all of the third dimension *were an extension of me* (created aspects coming from my multi-dimensional Self within), I often felt confused. In consciously understanding my dreams, I came to understand and accept that they were an energy from within me *that was creating my life*. I knew this because as I used the Dreamtime Method (interpreted my dream symbols as though each symbol was a physical aspect and ability of myself), my dream interpretations were always accurate, reflecting what was going on within my life. But how could my dreams and my subsequent created three-dimensional life, when they contained bad things, people or circumstances that I didn't like, really be being created and coming from me? And if this was true, how was I to accept and deal with that which I didn't like, as my own multi-dimensional energy?

The Triangle for Transforming— Your Multi-Dimensional Magic Wand Within

Over the years, I have come to understand that learning how to consciously interpret your dreams is only *one-half* of your dream work. Following your dream advice and *owning* your dreams and subsequent created three-dimensional life is another! As I consciously began to realize that my dreams were creating my three-dimensional reality, when I either had a dream I didn't like or saw someone, something, or some circumstance in my daily living that I could not accept as my own *reflection*, what I did was to try to *own* it in some way. But for me to "own" something as a part of myself within, I could really only do this in one way, that is, if what I was trying to own *had value* for me and my life, then I felt I could do it. I tried all kinds of ways to own dreams, other people, and circumstances that I didn't like, but the way that worked best for me was when I looked at what I was not owning (or denying as my own) that I had created, was as if it *had some value or was valuable to me and my life*.

In saying this, over the years I've come up with a tried and true *multi-dimensional technique* for owning dreams I do not like and/or three-dimensional energy in my life that I deny as mirroring myself. I have coined this multi-dimensional technique I developed as the *Triangle for Transforming*. This easy-to-do, but powerful, multi-dimensional technique allows you to integrate any *un-owned energy as your own multi-dimensional energy*. As you do the Triangle for Transforming technique, you integrate the energy you are denying as your own and transcend the three-dimensional illusion of separation which then transforms and merges the multi-dimensions of yourself within. The Triangle for Transforming is your *Magician's Wand* that I described back in Chapter One. Practicing and performing this simple, multi-dimensional technique changes everything!

The Triangle for Transforming technique can be used for "owning" any energy. The triangle can be used for accepting and owning dream energy and/or three-dimensional energy that you *do like* as your own. However, it is particularly effective in allowing yourself to *consciously own* any energy that you don't like, don't recognize "as

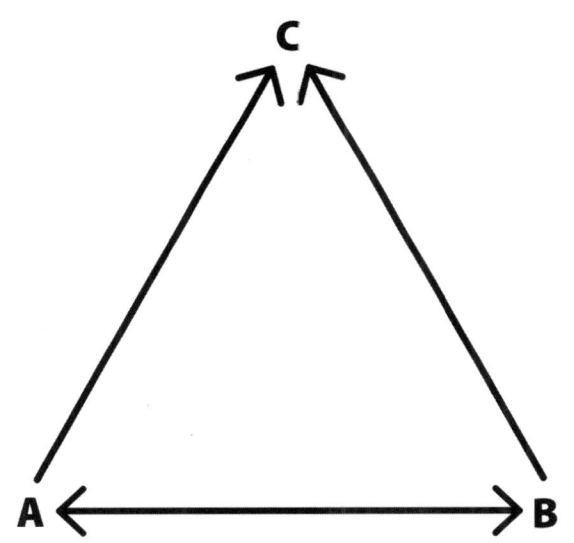

Figure 7.1

The Triangle "Within You" for Transforming

Point C =
Energy Conciousness of Your *Transformed*, Integrated and Whole Three-Dimensional / Multi-Dimensional Self

C

A   **B**

Point A =
Energy "Conciousness"
of Your Physical,
3-Dimensional Self

Point B =
Energy "Conciousness"
of Separation or
"Denied" Aspect of
Multi-Dimensional Self

you," and energy that you find difficult to accept as being a "multi-dimensional" aspect and part of your whole Self within.

I want you to now look at *figure 7.1*. This is the illustration of the Triangle *(within you)* for Transforming. In *figure 7.1*, I have the letter "A" (lower left point of the triangle) and want you to understand "A" as being representative of your present physical, three-dimensional Self.

The first step in the *Triangle for Transforming* is to bring to mind whatever "energy" (your dream, a three-dimensional person, a circumstance) you are unable to accept as being your mirror. Bringing to mind whatever you cannot accept as your mirror as a multi-dimensional aspect of you accomplishes just what you need to do! It brings to your conscious attention that which you are denying (positive or negative) as being your own multi-dimensional energy within.

Next you identify the negatives or positives of the energy that is troubling you as being your own. As you

Figure 7.1

The Triangle "Within You" for Transforming

Point C =
Energy Conciousness of Your *Transformed*, Integrated and Whole Three-Dimensional / Multi-Dimensional Self

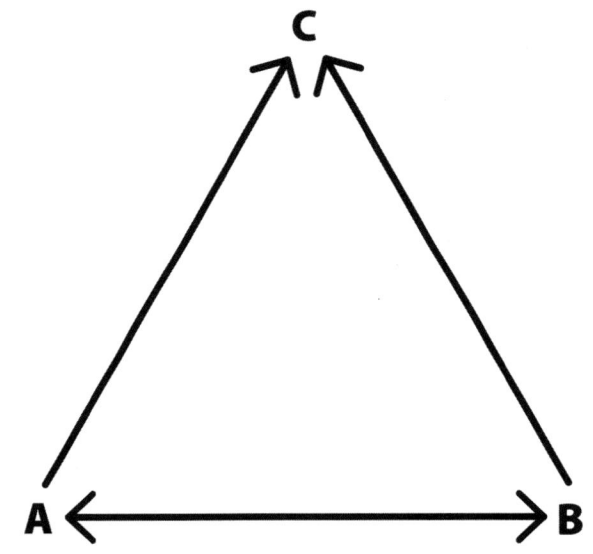

C

A **B**

Point A =
Energy "Conciousness"
of Your Physical,
3-Dimensional Self

Point B =
Energy "Conciousness"
of Separation or
"Denied" Aspect of
Multi-Dimensional Self

bring to mind whatever this energy is, think of the specifics of what you do or don't like about it. I have this "denied" negative or positive energy illustrated in *figure 7.1* with the letter "B" (lower right point of the Triangle).

As an example of my own "denied" multi-dimensional energy that I had had in a dream, several times my dream communicated to me that I was *an angry* person in my three-dimensional life. I was disturbed by the dream as I interpreted this understanding, since I didn't feel that in my waking reality I was an angry type of person. And not only that, but in my three-dimensional, everyday life, I didn't really like being around angry people.

As the next step in the Triangle for Transforming (which is what you will do as you use this technique), I tried to think of how *being* the energy I was denying or of me being an angry person may have ever *helped me* in my life, or how *being this energy* (angry) may assist, has assisted, or could be an "aid" for me now or in the future. In other words, I tried to think of whenever I had been angry, that the situation had turned out to be a *positive*. Thinking in this way, I was taking the seemingly *negative* emotion, circumstance, or person and seeing if being "the negative" could not only be useful to me, but a quality when needed to also assist me in my life. In this instance, I tried to think of what could be good about being the negative that I didn't want to accept as me, that of being an angry person.

As I thought about this, I thought of a time when I had arranged for painters to paint my house. They gave me a time frame to finish, yet day after day it dragged on. I finally got angry and called the owner of the painting business telling him that I needed to get the job done and was not going to pay him for "overtime" work! The owner of the company had no idea his workers were taking so long to get the job done and came right over. The job then got completed by the time I needed it and the owner of the company (for my trouble) even gave me a discount on the job! If I hadn't gotten *angry* and called the owner of the company, I don't know how much longer the situation would have gone on. And I certainly would not have received a discount! My getting angry with the painters and then calling the owner was not only appropriate in this situation, but turned out to be financially beneficial!

In trying to think of how being angry had *helped me in my life*, I then started to understand this emotion within me as something positive (a quality) versus a negative—which is what I typically had thought of "angry" people. I also became less upset by what my dream had communicated to me and really no longer felt it was an "issue" that caused conflict within me. I realized that being *"angry"* was an OK emotion and not something that I needed to deny. By doing this, I *owned* this aspect of myself within (the "angry" Terri) that I had created and did not recognize as me.

If you look back to *figure 7.1* on page 116, as I (point A) owned the behavior of being angry (point B), I *connected* those two aspects of myself within, transforming the "thinking" that I had going on within myself of me being "separate" from the angry Terri. Identifying and owning this denied aspect of myself immediately allowed me to integrate this multi-dimensional energy and *transform myself*, which is then shown as point C at the top of the Triangle.

In the above example, what was "valuable" and good about me dreaming of angry behavior and people wasn't the angry behavior or people. It was me recognizing the "angry Terri" that I might not have ever become aware of. The other valuable side of the coin in understanding and realizing that my dream symbols mirror my three-dimensional Self and life (being shown by me exhibiting anger in my dream) was that it came to my attention how I was being "angry" . . . with me! Bringing this behavior to my "waking" conscious Self made me more aware when I was not patient with myself and was being angry with myself. This valuable understanding allowed me to "consciously" lighten up on myself in my everyday life and give myself some compassion which also effectively helped to end any future angry dreams!

By taking the time to do the *Triangle for Transforming*, not only did I own this denied part of myself within which my dream and DreamSelf brought to my conscious attention, but I then never dreamed of being angry again! And because my dream energy was (and is) creating my three-dimensional Self and life, once I owned this denied aspect of myself (by doing the Triangle), angry people disappeared from my three-dimensional life. Angry people *disappeared* from my life because they were no longer mirroring to me this particular *un-owned and denied aspect* of my multi-dimensional Self! If I allowed the "angry Terri" to exist and to use it as a positive when I needed to, I didn't have to act it out in my everyday living nor have it mirrored back to me in other people, circumstances, or my dreams.

Remember, if you don't own that which is yours, the "un-owned" energy will stay in place just as it is now, *separate from you.* When you deny yourself, that aspect (of you) will continue to present itself in your dreams and subsequent life because it wants to be recognized and acknowledged within your everyday consciousness. This multi-dimensional aspect of you wants to be accepted and loved as your own Self because *it is a part of you that you have created* and is "reflective" of the total multi-dimensional "you" within. This is why, once you own the dream, the person, the thing, or the situation—and *accept it as part of yourself*—it will no longer continue to be mirrored back to you; it will be integrated into your "waking three-dimensional consciousness" as being *the total* of your multi-dimensional Self within, which it is!

In summary, the steps for consciously doing the "Triangle" are:

➺ Identify the energy in your dream (or everyday life) that you want (or need) to "own" as your own Self. Really look at what it is that makes you feel negative about the energy. If the energy in your dream is positive, but you feel uncomfortable about it mirroring you, identify that energy.

➺ Think of how this energy has in the past or present or could possibly in the future help and assist you in your life. Try to look at how this energy may be perceived by you as being of value to assist you within yourself and life.

After you do the "Triangle," try to be *aware* of how this energy you have identified doesn't present itself as an issue in your dreams or within you and your three-dimensional life anymore. Try to understand that, after doing the Triangle, this denied aspect of yourself has now been integrated within—creating the consciousness of a *new transformed and whole "you."*

Freedom from Fear

What you are really doing as you "own" all of the dimensions of your Self Within (i.e., your everyday three-dimensional Self and the non-physical dimensions of yourself within, which are your dreams) is consciously bringing to your awareness your *already created* whole multi-dimensional Self. And this is excellent news for you and your life!

This may sound like a lot of work for you, but let me tell you, the rewards within you and your life will be many! As you do your dream work and bring to your conscious attention your total Self, your DreamSelf Within, you create *freedom*. When you interpret your dreams multi-dimensionally, consciously connecting that information to your every-day Self and life, you allow your life decisions for yourself to be based on your inner Light and compass versus being based on the created every day, three-dimensional *emotion of fear*. And, as you create freedom of your Spirit, you *feel* integrated, lighter and more whole. That means that situations *work for you* in your life! Everything changes and life gets easier, more fun, more prosperous, and more *harmonic*.

As you use the Dreamtime Method and "think" of yourself as "multi-dimensional" or acknowledge that the third dimension is the slower vibrating energy coming from the power of your own unlimited 10th dimensional Self within, you then realize that *you are the power within who has in the past and is now in the present creating your three-dimensional Self and life* and that you, in reality, can create anything you want!

Dreamtime Method Recap

Dreamers, congratulations! You have completed your instruction on the Dreamtime Method! For your final review, I will now give you an overview of the Dreamtime Method along with some final thoughts.

The Dreamtime Method of dream interpretation is learning to *think* as your multi-dimensional DreamSelf Within does, the part of you within that creates and communicates your dreams. When you "think" just as the part of yourself that creates your dreams symbols, *you receive an absolutely accurate interpretation of your dream!*

The Dreamtime Method for "thinking" as your DreamSelf Within does is this:

➻ You start by taking the normal three-dimensional definition and understanding for the dream symbol.

➻ You then think of that understanding as your DreamSelf Within does, which is that you are the actual physical, three-dimensional definition/energy of your dream symbol. By "thinking" in this way, you interpret your dream symbol's definition and

119

understanding as your DreamSelf Within does, which is as though your dream symbol's meaning is a "physical aspect, power, and ability" that you now three-dimensionally have and possess from within.

⇥ As you think in this way, the information that you receive gives you an absolutely accurate interpretation of your dream symbol.

To interpret your dream in total, do the following:

⇥ Write your dream out in chronological sequence or in the order that things occurred in your dream.

⇥ Next, use the Dreamtime Method to interpret each dream symbol. Write your Dreamtime interpretation/meaning in parenthesis next to the dream symbol

⇥ After you have done this, add the dream interpretations together in the order they occurred in your dream to receive the complete thoughts of your DreamSelf Within and get an absolute accurate interpretation of your dream.

A key to remember when interpreting your dream is that your dream symbols as the thoughts of your all-knowing DreamSelf Within not only tell and relate, but also as energy, create in the third-dimension!

⇥ Your dream symbols, as a communication from your DreamSelf, not only give you intelligent information and guidance for your life, but also as your own inner 10th dimensional "light energy" attract in more and similar energy to provide the physical, three-dimensional way (energy) to accomplish and resolve whatever your dream is addressing. So be sure after interpreting your dream meaning to be on the alert and look for the energy to come into your life to assist with whatever your dream is communicating!

Your Power to Dream

Interpreting your dreams transforms you. How? Your dreams teach you *consciously* that you are the *Creator of Your Life*. As you learn to interpret your dreams using the Dreamtime Method and activate your DreamSelf's consciousness—your Spiritual Sight into your three-dimensional life, *you will never be the same*. The reason is that as you open your multi-dimensional dream door, you bring your clairvoyant, telepathic DreamSelf, your Magician Within, into your everyday Self and life!

As you consciously learn to interpret your dreams and know what they mean, you will sense that you have come from your *future* (your 10th Dimensional DreamSelf Within) to alter, change, and raise the vibration of your physical, three-dimensional Self *in your now*. This understanding says that you have come from your own *multi-dimensional future* to awaken and unfold your *Spiritual Self and Spiritual Sight* in the third dimension which not only alters your now, but the future multi-dimensions of yourself that are simultaneously occurring! And the way that you are accomplishing this, the connection and pathway is by interpreting *your multi-dimensional dreams*.

Your dreams are your everyday reminders that all of the power that ever was and ever will be is here within you now. Your dreams remind you that you are a *Divine Being* of unlimited energy and potential within! And, as you bring your DreamSelf's vision, your dreams actively into your three-dimensional life, your formula for living will be this. In all that you experience, you will be fully present, multi-dimensionally able, and living *in your now*. As you learn to interpret your dreams and realize that all that surrounds you now in the third dimension is a reflection of the multi-dimensional you that lies within, you will enter into a new journey of Self—*Your Conscious Journey into Wholeness*.

Right now, there is a beautiful spiraling of energy from the Milky Way Galaxy stars that is descending into the energy of our magnificent Sun. The Sun's energy continues on, vibrating and melding into the breath-taking blue-green energy of our planet Earth. And what I see next is the spiraling magnificent energy . . . of you!

Thank you for taking this exciting conscious journey into wholeness with me to open your Spiritual Sight Within. I hope you have enjoyed my book, *Dreamtime Dream Interpretation*, and learned a lot about yourself. You will be learning even more as you continue on now and use the Dreamtime Method to accurately interpret your own dreams.

DREAMTIME AFFIRMATION

I Will and Intend this glorious day

to live fully in the Present Moment, my Now . . .

In the deepest vibrational frequency of healing Love, Light, and Harmony

for myself and the *"rest of myself"* . . .

As I am guided with Knowing, Confidence, and Sovereignty

By my Divine Multi-Dimensional DreamSelf that lies within

About the Author

Terri became interested in dreams twenty years ago. Finding the available resources lacking to learn to interpret her own dreams, she created the Dreamtime Method which allowed her to interpret her dreams with great accuracy. Sixteen years ago, she created her website **www.dreaminterpretation.com** to test the Dreamtime methodology for accuracy on other people. Since then, she has been interpreting dreams using the Dreamtime Method, which has resulted in amazing testimonials from thousands of people all over the world. The feedback has been that not only did Terri interpret their dreams accurately, but that her interpretations exactly matched what was going on in the dreamers' lives! The dreamers were all amazed and inspired at the guidance and information Terri could give them just from interpreting their dreams using the Dreamtime Method.

Terri teaches the step-by-step Dreamtime Method in this book, *Dreamtime Dream Interpretation,* and in her Dreamtime Dream Interpretation workshops.

The Author lives with her husband Dave and Golden Retriever, Cody, in Colorado.

My Dreamtime Dream Dictionary

My Dreamtime Dream Dictionary

My Dreamtime Dream Dictionary

My Dreamtime Dream Dictionary

My Dreamtime Dream Dictionary

My Dreamtime Dream Dictionary

My Dreamtime Dream Dictionary

My Dreamtime Dream Dictionary

My Dreamtime Dream Dictionary

My Dreamtime Dream Dictionary

Dreamtime Method Template

- Using the Dreamtime Method, the normal, three-dimensional definition of

  a _____ could be understood as a

  _____.

- I then think of this definition/meaning as my DreamSelf within *thinks of*

  it, which is as though the dream symbol of a_____

  is now a "physical aspect and ability" of my own three-dimensional

  energy that comes from within.

- As I think of myself *being* the energy of the three-dimensional_____

  _____, the interpretation

  that I get from *"thinking"* as my DreamSelf Within does is that for the

  dream symbol of a_____,

  my DreamSelf wants to communicate information to me about

  _____

  _____

  _____

  within my everyday Self and life.

Dreamtime Method Template

- **Using the Dreamtime Method, the normal, three-dimensional definition of a** _____ **could be understood as a**

  _____ .

- **I then think of this definition/meaning as my DreamSelf within** _thinks of it_, **which is as though the dream symbol of a**_____

  is now a "physical aspect and ability" of my own three-dimensional

  energy that comes from within.

- **As I think of myself** _being_ **the energy of the three-dimensional**_____

  _____, **the interpretation**

  that I get from _"thinking"_ **as my DreamSelf Within does is that for the**

  dream symbol of a_____ ,

  my DreamSelf wants to communicate information to me about

  _____

  _____

  _____

  within my everyday Self and life.

Dreamtime Method Template

- **Using the Dreamtime Method, the normal, three-dimensional definition of**

  a _____ **could be understood as a**

  _____ .

- **I then think of this definition/meaning as my DreamSelf within _thinks of_**

  _it_, which is as though the dream symbol of a_____

  is now a "physical aspect and ability" of my own three-dimensional

  energy that comes from within.

- **As I think of myself _being_ the energy of the three-dimensional**_____

  _____ **, the interpretation**

  that I get from "_thinking_" as my DreamSelf Within does is that for the

  dream symbol of a_____ **,**

  my DreamSelf wants to communicate information to me about

  _____

  _____

  _____

  within my everyday Self and life.

Dreamtime Method Template

- **Using the Dreamtime Method, the normal, three-dimensional definition of**

  a _____ **could be understood as a**

  _____ **.**

- **I then think of this definition/meaning as my DreamSelf within *thinks of***

  ***it*, which is as though the dream symbol of a**_____

  is now a "physical aspect and ability" of my own three-dimensional

  energy that comes from within.

- **As I think of myself *being* the energy of the three-dimensional**_____

  _____**, the interpretation**

  that I get from *"thinking"* as my DreamSelf Within does is that for the

  dream symbol of a_____ **,**

  my DreamSelf wants to communicate information to me about

  _____

  _____

  _____

  within my everyday Self and life.

Dreamtime Method Template

- Using the Dreamtime Method, the normal, three-dimensional definition of

  a _____ could be understood as a

  _____.

- I then think of this definition/meaning as my DreamSelf within *thinks of*

  it, which is as though the dream symbol of a_____

  is now a "physical aspect and ability" of my own three-dimensional

  energy that comes from within.

- As I think of myself *being* the energy of the three-dimensional_____

  _____, the interpretation

  that I get from "*thinking*" as my DreamSelf Within does is that for the

  dream symbol of a_____ ,

  my DreamSelf wants to communicate information to me about

  _____

  _____

  _____

  within my everyday Self and life.

Dreamtime Method Template

- **Using the Dreamtime Method, the normal, three-dimensional definition of a _____ could be understood as a**

  _____.

- **I then think of this definition/meaning as my DreamSelf within *thinks of it*, which is as though the dream symbol of a_____ is now a "physical aspect and ability" of my own three-dimensional energy that comes from within.**

- **As I think of myself *being* the energy of the three-dimensional_____ _____, the interpretation that I get from "*thinking*" as my DreamSelf Within does is that for the dream symbol of a_____ , my DreamSelf wants to communicate information to me about**

  _____

  _____

  _____

  within my everyday Self and life.

Dreamtime Method Template

- **Using the Dreamtime Method, the normal, three-dimensional definition of a** _____ **could be understood as a**

  _____.

- **I then think of this definition/meaning as my DreamSelf within _thinks of it_, which is as though the dream symbol of a**_____

  is now a "physical aspect and ability"of my own three-dimensional

  energy that comes from within.

- **As I think of myself _being_ the energy of the three-dimensional**_____

  _____**, the interpretation**

  that I get from _"thinking"_ as my DreamSelf Within does is that for the

  dream symbol of a_____ **,**

  my DreamSelf wants to communicate information to me about

  _____

  _____

  _____

  within my everyday Self and life.

Dreamtime Method Template

- Using the Dreamtime Method, the normal, three-dimensional definition of

  a _____ could be understood as a

  _____.

- I then think of this definition/meaning as my DreamSelf within *thinks of*

  it, which is as though the dream symbol of a_____

  is now a "physical aspect and ability"of my own three-dimensional

  energy that comes from within.

- As I think of myself *being* the energy of the three-dimensional_____

  _____, the interpretation

  that I get from *"thinking"* as my DreamSelf Within does is that for the

  dream symbol of a_____ ,

  my DreamSelf wants to communicate information to me about

  _____

  _____

  _____

  within my everyday Self and life.

Dreamtime Method Template

- **Using the Dreamtime Method, the normal, three-dimensional definition of**

  a _____ **could be understood as a**

  _____ **.**

- **I then think of this definition/meaning as my DreamSelf within *thinks of***

  it, which is as though the dream symbol of a_____

  is now a "physical aspect and ability" of my own three-dimensional

  energy that comes from within.

- **As I think of myself *being* the energy of the three-dimensional**_____

  _____**, the interpretation**

  that I get from *"thinking"* as my DreamSelf Within does is that for the

  dream symbol of a_____ **,**

  my DreamSelf wants to communicate information to me about

  _____

  _____

  _____

  within my everyday Self and life.

Dreamtime Method Template

- **Using the Dreamtime Method, the normal, three-dimensional definition of a** _____ **could be understood as a**

  _____ .

- **I then think of this definition/meaning as my DreamSelf within** _thinks of_

  _it_, **which is as though the dream symbol of a**_____

  is now a "physical aspect and ability" of my own three-dimensional

  energy that comes from within.

- **As I think of myself** _being_ **the energy of the three-dimensional**_____

  _____ **, the interpretation**

  that I get from _"thinking"_ **as my DreamSelf Within does is that for the**

  dream symbol of a_____ **,**

  my DreamSelf wants to communicate information to me about

  _____

  _____

  _____

  within my everyday Self and life.

Dreamtime Dream Journal

Date:

Dear_____,

(Write your dream out here.)

My DreamSelf says that within my thinking and thought creating my now . . .

(Write your Dreamtime Dream Interpretation here.)

What happened that day:

Dreamtime Dream Journal

Date:

Dear_____,

(Write your dream out here.)

My DreamSelf says that within my thinking and thought creating my now . . .

(Write your Dreamtime Dream Interpretation here.)

What happened that day:

Dreamtime Dream Journal

Date:
Dear_____,
(Write your dream out here.)

My DreamSelf says that within my thinking and thought creating my now . . .
(Write your Dreamtime Dream Interpretation here.)

What happened that day:

Dreamtime Dream Journal

Date:

Dear_____,

(Write your dream out here.)

My DreamSelf says that within my thinking and thought creating my now . . .

(Write your Dreamtime Dream Interpretation here.)

What happened that day:

Dreamtime Dream Journal

Date:

Dear_____**,**

(Write your dream out here.)

My DreamSelf says that within my thinking and thought creating my now . . .

(Write your Dreamtime Dream Interpretation here.)

What happened that day:

Dreamtime Dream Journal

Date:

Dear_____,

(Write your dream out here.)

My DreamSelf says that within my thinking and thought creating my now ...

(Write your Dreamtime Dream Interpretation here.)

What happened that day:

Dreamtime Dream Journal

Date:

Dear_____,

(Write your dream out here.)

My DreamSelf says that within my thinking and thought creating my now . . .

(Write your Dreamtime Dream Interpretation here.)

What happened that day:

Dreamtime Dream Journal

Date:

Dear_____,

(Write your dream out here.)

My DreamSelf says that within my thinking and thought creating my now . . .

(Write your Dreamtime Dream Interpretation here.)

What happened that day:

Dreamtime Dream Journal

Date:

Dear_____,

(Write your dream out here.)

My DreamSelf says that within my thinking and thought creating my now . . .

(Write your Dreamtime Dream Interpretation here.)

What happened that day:

Dreamtime Dream Journal

Date:

Dear_____,

(Write your dream out here.)

My DreamSelf says that within my thinking and thought creating my now . . .

(Write your Dreamtime Dream Interpretation here.)

What happened that day:

INDEX

Dreamtime Product Ordering

All of the following Dreamtime products can be ordered through the website: www.dreaminterpretation.com

The Dreamtime products that are available include:

- The Dreamtime Dream Interpretation Book
- The Dreamtime Dream Interpretation Audio Book - CD
- The Dreamtime Dream Journal Notebook
  (pre-printed dream journal pages for recording your dreams)

Workshops

Terri also presents *Dreamtime Dream Interpretation Workshops* for learning the Dreamtime Method of interpreting your own dreams. To check on scheduled work-shops or to contact the author about giving a workshop, please go to: www.dreaminterpretation.com

Thank You!